Into the Abyss

The Memoirs of a Paranormal Adventurer

Travis McHenry

Into the Abyss: The Memoirs of a Paranormal Adventurer
© 2006 Travis McHenry

SECOND EDITION © 2010
ISBN 978-0-557-52601-7

Cover design by Travis McHenry
Cover photo *Travis with a Gigantopithecus Mandible* by Cathryn McHenry

To my wife Cathryn

TABLE OF CONTENTS

ACKNOWLEDGEMENTS

I would like to thank the following individuals and organizations for assisting me in the research and investigations which led me to write this book:

George Morin, Neil Whitmoyer, Sam Taylor, Rick Fisher, Eric Altman, Stan Gordon, Robert W. Morgan, Grover Krantz, Peter Byrne, Chris Murphy, William Draganis, Mr. G. Hoke, Bob Willis, Mike Frizzell, Scott Ditmer, Stanton Friedman, Bruce Cornet, Joe Decker, Philip Karns, Butch Hunt, Emily Honts, Maria Monroe, Janie Kishbaugh, Laura Salvucci, J. Vitkoski, Michelle Gachette, Bob Schott, Doug Ruckle, Jennifer Lindner, the Paranormal Society of Pennsylvania, the Pennsylvania Bigfoot Society, the American Anthropological Research Foundation, the Botetourt County Historical Society, the College of Physicians of Philadelphia, and Harvard University Library.

I must also extend a special thanks to my wife Cathryn for supporting my paranormal research and being a good sport at paranormal conventions.

INTRODUCTION

The vast majority of books on the paranormal have been written with the primary purpose of educating the general public about paranormal phenomena, and showcasing the investigator's work. This is a noble goal, but there should also be some literature available for the seasoned investigator to further their understanding of paranormal theories. Too many authors and publishers are focused on pleasing the public and are unconcerned with advancing the scientific method beyond the point of simply recording data. This book aims to do just that.

Some of the theories I have developed go against the grain of what is considered acceptable to the community of paranormal investigators. That's fine; otherwise, I would have no reason to compile them together and release them in this format. I strongly encourage the reader to tear apart the theories discussed here and then put them back together to see if they truly hold any water. I do not have all the answers. To be honest, I don't think anyone does, but my research has reached the point where I have drawn certain conclusions, and now release them for scrutiny by my peers. If I were a conventional scientist, each of the following chapters could be released one at a time in a peer-reviewed journal. Unfortunately, there is no truly respected medium for paranormal investigators to utilize for this purpose.

Focusing this volume towards knowledgeable researchers has allowed me to avoid retelling the same hackneyed stories that anyone involved in paranormal investigation has heard a million times. For example, I do not offer a multi-page discourse on the Patterson Film because it has been thoroughly covered by believers and skeptics. There are numerous books, websites, and documentary films dedicated to proving or disproving the film's authenticity. If you have seen the Patterson Film, you either consider that it may be real, or you dismiss it completely. My take on the film would not benefit the Bigfoot researcher community in any way. It is for similar reasons that I have not bothered to dwell on such famous incidents as the Roswell UFO crash, instead focusing on the Kecksburg UFO crash, about which very little has been written.

You will notice the names of many researchers and investigators throughout this book, and I have named them for a reason. Without the cooperation of my fellow paranormal investigators, none of my theories could have ever been developed. There is so much competition between researchers; everyone loses when investigators fail to share their methods and data with others. I suppose that I would like to close by encouraging other researchers to continue to share their information through websites, books, and even their own documentary films.

TRAVIS McHENRY

CHAPTER 1

Gorillas in Our Midst

Sasquatch, more commonly known as Bigfoot, has been sighted tens of thousands of times over the last two hundred years. Modern reports of Bigfoot are consistent with a similar creature known as the Yeti which is thought to inhabit the Himalayan Mountain range. Both creatures average seven and a half feet in height and have an average reported weight of 600 to 1,000 pounds. They can have fur ranging in color from dark brown to snowy gray, or in rare cases even stark white. These creatures are said to be heavily built, apelike, and hairy, but with facial features resembling those of a human. They are reportedly able to communicate with grunts, cries, whistles, and mimicked animal sounds. Footprints, the most prolific evidence of their existence, are fifteen inches on average.

A common question I get is "How many of these creatures are there living in the United States?" To be honest, although every Bigfoot researcher has their own population estimate, based on their own interpretation of the available evidence, no one can quote these numbers with any certainty. My personal estimate is that there are somewhere around 2,000 Bigfoot creatures living throughout the continental U.S. and Canada.

Another question that many people ask is "What does Bigfoot eat?" Bigfoot appears to be completely omnivorous, but there is the possibility that the creatures resort to a singularly carnivorous diet where there is no vegetation available, scavenging the forest for carcasses, and adopting a predatory posture when necessary. When food is available, a Bigfoot could easily survive off the same diet as a bear. Berries, apples, small animals, fish; basically, anything it can find. If Bigfoot is equipped with a hind gut fermenter (as it probably is) then it would be able to effectively digest vegetation and gain increased energy proportional to its digesting/fermenting time.

The possibility has also been raised that Bigfoot is able to survive on a diet of pine needles during the winter months. This may seem absurd, but the practice is actually quite common among poor North Koreans. The Natural Health Foodstuff Company which operates under the North Korean Ministry of Forestry has developed pine needle tea and liquor, both of which are advertised as having health benefits. The practice of boiling and eating pine needles was also promoted by the Soviets for isolated Siberian peasants.

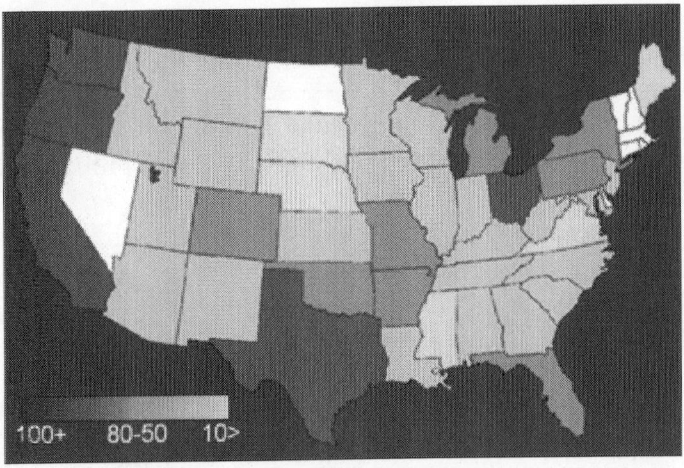

Figure 1. Map of U.S. Bigfoot sightings by state.

WHAT IS IT?

First, I'd like to review some of the different theories about what Bigfoot is and carefully explain why I don't think they sufficiently answer our question as to Bigfoot's identity.

Based on eyewitness reports, some Bigfoot creatures have been known to exhibit paranormal behavior. These accounts are very rare, totaling only three percent of the total reported encounters. One report that I am aware of involves a Bigfoot creature being only partially visible from the waist up and then disappearing into thin air. These reports may seem very unlikely to most Bigfoot researchers, but when the people reporting them are sane and rational individuals, then we must take their sightings at face value and begin to examine the plausibility of what they saw.

In the case of a "ghostly Bigfoot," I would like to offer this possibility. Some humans die, and there are ghosts of them remaining, some animals die, and there are ghosts of them remaining; so if Bigfoot is something between a human and an animal, then why wouldn't some of them leave a ghostly presence behind when they die?

One of the things you have to ask yourself when you read an encounter of a Bigfoot exhibiting behavior that you might consider paranormal, for instance, appearing and disappearing into thin air, or being only semi-invisible is: Is this something that is normal behavior for a ghostly being? If my great-grandfather were to appear before me and then suddenly disappear, would I assume that all human beings have that special ability? No, of course not. I would realize that I had just seen the ghost of my great-grandfather and react accordingly. It's exactly the same with Bigfoot. To illustrate this more completely, I'm going to use one of Rick Fisher's stories.

Rick Fisher, founder of the Paranormal Society of Pennsylvania and longtime Bigfoot researcher, once saw what he equated to a Bigfoot on a lonely back road in Pennsylvania. It was February of 2002 and Rick was by himself driving down Pennsylvania Route 23 near Lancaster when he saw a strange figure, which looked like a man dressed in black, walking along the edge of the road. Being an inquisitive person, Rick slowed the car and put his headlights on what he thought was a person. As his car crept closer to this lone figure, Rick could see it more clearly. It appeared to be a Bigfoot, but like none he had ever heard of before.

The creature was about five feet tall, covered in dark hair, and, oddly, as thin as a stick. "The legs were so thin, I was amazed it could stand or walk on them," Rick later stated. He continued to follow this bizarre creature, trying to deduce what it might be. It was too thin and too short to be a Bigfoot, but it resembled Bigfoot in the respect that it was covered with hair and walking upright. This creature kept walking slowly along the side of the road for several minutes and then it stopped and turned towards Rick.

"It had two bright yellow eyes," Rick said, "then it vanished. It didn't run off into the woods, just vanished before my eyes." At first, he was very frightened, not knowing where the creature could have disappeared to. "I didn't know where it went, it could have reappeared there in the car with me." Feeling uneasy and slightly confused, Rick decided to leave the scene as quickly as he could. When later telling the story about the mysterious being, Rick could only equate it to Bigfoot, although he was the first to say that he had no idea what it actually was.

That event could lead some to ask the question, "Oh, I wonder if all Bigfoot have that ability?" Consider this: What if during one particularly unpleasant winter, there was a Bigfoot creature that was emaciated and starving to death due to a lack of food, and this Bigfoot was walking up and down the lonely stretch of road, dying of hunger while looking for food. And finally, one day, it did die, and then Rick Fisher just happened to be driving along when its ghost was repeating that exact same activity, walking up and down the side of the road. There is also the possibility that this particular creature is something totally different; the result of a demonic presence, for example.

What I'm trying to suggest here is that all Bigfoot are not ghosts, but a select few of the Bigfoot that have died may be ghostly beings, and may still be living on either as intelligent or non-intelligent entities. One other thing you need to keep in mind is that there can't be a ghost of something that was never alive. There are no people who were born as ghosts. It must, therefore, be the same with Bigfoot.

Figure 2. Artist's conception of the creature Rick Fisher saw on a lonesome Pennsylvania back road. *Courtesy John Weaver and Rick Fisher.*

15

Many investigators have found strands of Bigfoot hair. This hair has been analyzed and in several cases, the scientist conducting the analysis was unable to match it to any known animal, but it is similar to primate hair. The lunatic fringe of Bigfoot research would have you believe that Bigfoot is able to materialize and dematerialize, and is closer to an interdimensional person than a flesh and blood creature.

However, apparitions do not leave clumps of hair behind, and even if they did, when the being disappears, their clumps of hair would assuredly follow. If a Bigfoot could simply dematerialize or enter another dimension, or turn themselves invisible (yes, all of these traits have been attributed to Bigfoot by the lunatic fringe) then why did the creature in the Patterson Film take the time to walk away into the woods? Why didn't it just vanish before the camera? The sad part is that I know members of this fringe will actually contact me to explain in detail the reason the creature chose not to vanish, and worse, when I ask how they know this, they will undoubtedly respond, "Bigfoot told me, of course."

There are a number of instances where a Bigfoot creature has been sighted around the same time, or in the vicinity of, a UFO. This begs the question, is Bigfoot an alien being, or is it connected to the UFO phenomena? If aliens from outer space, or whatever these UFOs are, are interested in earthly life such as human beings and cattle, then why wouldn't they also be interested in a Bigfoot? There's no reason that they wouldn't.

If you were looking at a field of cattle late one night, and you saw a UFO hover over and a beam of light emitted from the bottom of the craft, and one of the cows was carried up into the flying craft, would you assume that all cows are aliens? That's ridiculous, of course not. You'd say, "Look at that, we'll probably read about a cattle mutilation in the paper tomorrow." Scientific interest on the part of the UFO occupants is one possible way of explaining why UFOs are sometimes seen in close proximity to Bigfoot creatures.

The other possibility is that some alien species just happen to resemble the Bigfoot creatures. And if you look at the actual sightings of purported alien beings, fourteen percent of witnesses claim that the alien creature they saw resembled a hairy, upright mammal. If a Bigfoot researcher were to see such a being walking through the woods, they would automatically assume that it was a Bigfoot, but if a UFO appeared in the sky and beamed it up, the researcher wouldn't think that all Bigfoot creatures are from another planet.

So what we're facing here is a case of mistaken identity, that's all. There are these hairy, upright walking beings out there that people assume are Bigfoot, when in reality, they are, or could be aliens from another planet. I'm not saying all of these types of aliens exist, but these bizarre sightings require an explanation, and I think this is the best, most reasonable one.

A very popular theory in the Bigfoot research community is that this creature is some form of proto-human, such as a Neanderthal or a relic *Homo erectus*, but I think this is highly unlikely. Proponents of this theory cite Bigfoot's bipedal nature, its upright walking posture, and the numerous eyewitness reports which mention the creature's human-like facial features. While it would be a treat for evolutionists to prove Darwin's theory correct, I do not think proto-human is the proper classification for Bigfoot.

The Neanderthal was not covered with hair, and Bigfoot is. A typical male grew no taller than about six feet, and weighed a maximum of two hundred pounds; and this is true for all of the human ancestors, in fact, proto-humans get shorter and lighter the farther back in time you go. Also, the Neanderthal and other proto-humans possessed very useful abilities that it would not want to give up. The ability to use fire, for example, and using weapons to hunt and also stone tool craftsmanship. Bigfoot creatures have never been witnessed utilizing any of these abilities, and why would you give them up once you had them? It doesn't make very much sense. There is also evidence that Neanderthal wore animal skins as clothing which Bigfoot obviously doesn't need to do because it's covered with hair.

This brings me to the final possibility for the proper classification of Bigfoot, and it is one that was first put forth by noted physical anthropologist Doctor Grover Krantz, author of the book *Bigfoot Sasquatch Evidence*. He theorized that the Bigfoot was not a living fossil Neanderthal, but instead a prehistoric ape called *Gigantopithecus blacki*. The eyewitness descriptions of Bigfoot match perfectly with that of *Gigantopithecus:* a seven to eight-foot-tall, ape-like creature covered with hair that walked upright. *Gigantopithecus* was known to have co-existed with *Homo erectus*, and the most recent evidence suggests that it died out only 100,000 years ago, which is relatively recent in our historical timeline. Don't forget that the Coelacanth was thought to have gone extinct more than 65 million years ago, and scientists were definitely proven wrong on that account.

The primary range of *Gigantopithecus*, so far as we can tell from fossil evidence, was China and Indo-China. Both the Orangutan and the Giant Panda shared the habitat of the *Gigantopithecus*, and still inhabit that region to this day; there is a chance that some portion of the *Gigantopithecus* species survived to the present day. Incidentally, this is a region where three different types of giant ape-man are reported to exist. The Orang-pendek is believed to make its home in Indo-China, while China is where both the Yaren, and the Yeti, most famously, are known to live.

Because *Gigantopithecus* co-existed with *Homo erectus*, it would've learned to avoid those proto-humans because *erectus* would've been more intelligent than *Gigantopithecus*. Also, more than likely, the two species were in competition for food sources; and there is the further possibility that *erectus* hunted *Gigantopithecus*. So in order to survive, it would've had to be intelligent enough to hide in remote areas, away from *Homo erectus* and later *Homo sapiens*. This is behavior that

Gigantopithecus is still exhibiting to this day. It's doing the exact same thing it was 100,000 years ago. However, I'm not suggesting that Bigfoot is simply a dumb ape. They obviously have increased in intelligence; so have dolphins, chimps, and pigs. If you put the intelligence of a dolphin in the body of a gorilla, you've got an approximation of a Bigfoot.

  Gigantopithecus' diet was the same as a Giant Panda, primarily bamboo. But they supplemented their diet with other sources of food as well, just like the Giant Panda; with berries, leaves, roots, fish, and animal life. After the species migrated to North America they were able to live off the same diet as American bears. It is not a coincidence to this author that bamboo is prevalent in the Pacific Northwest, and that the early *Gigantopithecus* probably followed the bamboo growth leading to its present habitation. It is also worth noting that the Mountain Gorillas of Rwanda subside on a healthy diet of bamboo shoots in addition to local foliage.

  People always ask why we don't ever find the remains of a dead Bigfoot. Besides the fact that the remains of animals that die natural deaths in the wild rarely last longer than a few days due to scavengers feasting on them, it is no matter of coincidence that the only traces of *Gigantopithecus* are fossilized teeth and jaws. My conclusion is that Bigfoot is a modern-day flesh and blood *Gigantopithecus blacki* that has no paranormal abilities, and no direct relationship to UFOs or aliens.

  The hypothetical migration of *Gigantopithecus* out of Asia can account for Bigfoot sightings not just in the United States, but all over the world. In the creature's original habitat it is known as the Yeti, the Yaren, and the Orang Pendek. Moving south into Australia, the creature is known as the Yowie. Human beings made this exact same migration and became the aboriginal tribes that are found on that continent. To the north, in Russia, they are Almas. Crossing the Bering Straight Land Bridge and entering North America, which, incidentally, is how early *Homo sapiens* arrived on the continent, they are known as the Sasquatch in the Pacific Northwest, and the Skunk Ape in the American South East. If you compare this with human migration patterns from the same time period, you see that they are identical.

DIFFERENT TRACKS

One problem that has long frustrated Bigfoot researchers is what seem to be inconsistencies in the footprint evidence which Bigfoot is said to leave behind. There have been numerous photographs and casts made of three-toed tracks that have been found all over the East Coast of the United States. I myself once found such a track.

In late January 2000, I was hiking through Ricketts Glen State Park, in Northern Pennsylvania. It was a bitterly cold day, and there was a heavy layer of snow on the ground. Due to the fact that many hunters live in the area, and ice fishing is popular, the park stays open all year. However, during the winter months, the hiking trails are closed to the general public, and only trained climbers are permitted to hike the rough terrain.

At that time, I had been climbing for close to a year, and had made many trips to the State Park in the summer months, so I felt confident that I knew which parts were dangerous and thus to be avoided. Because it was so cold, and a weekday, there was no one to be found throughout the entire park. This was what I was hoping for, as I like to be alone during my long hikes. As I started into the woods, the wind picked up and it became extremely cold. I could only take my hands out of my gloves for a moment before they became totally numb.

The path to the top of the highland trail was not an easy one, especially since there was ice over everything. I continued on, pausing only occasionally to catch my breath and take a picture or two of the scenic surroundings. After hiking for nearly an hour, I came to the steep dry streambed that I have

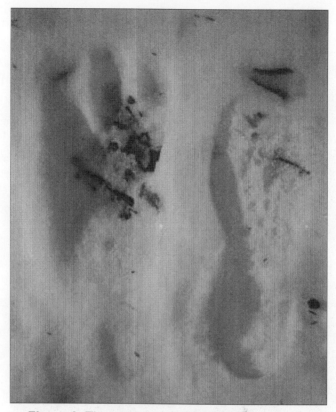

Figure 3. Three toed track found by the author in Rickett's Glen, Pennsylvania.

often climbed. Due to the cold, a thick sheet of ice covered the entire bed, and I had to walk along the outside edge.

Halfway up the bed, I started to notice odd footprints. They were three-toed, but they were all wind-blown and most were incomplete. They reminded me of the footprints seen on *The Legend of Boggy Creek*, but because I didn't see a perfect one, I didn't bother to take any pictures. That was until I reached a small plateau on the incline. There in the snow was a perfect three-toed footprint. It was exactly what I had seen in the movie. I placed my foot (size 11 ½) in the snow beside it and left a footprint for comparison; the three-toed footprint was only a little bigger than mine. I snapped a picture and continued to the top of the trail.

At the top of the trail, there was a large rock formation, which I have often climbed on, covered with ice and very treacherous. I decided to try to get to the top anyway, even though I was wearing bulky hiking boots instead of slim climbing shoes. Almost to the top of the formation, I slipped, and was saved from certain injury by grabbing onto a tree that was growing out of the rock. As I fell, my knee banged against the rock and sent me into severe pain. I shook this off, steadied myself and continued climbing. Safely on top of the rock, I checked my knee (which had a large cut, and I still have the scar) and sat to think about what I had seen on the trail.

I had always had a sneaking suspicion that there was some kind of bi-pedal creature stalking through the State Park, but I never had any solid evidence. Finally, it was in my possession. I continued to scan the vast wilderness before me, naively hoping for a glance at the upright-walking creature, but found none.

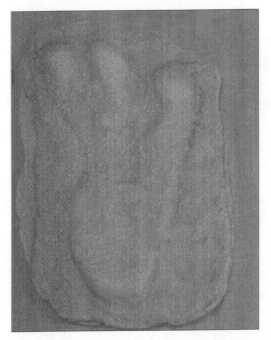

Figure 4. Three toed track Stan Gordon found in Pennsylvania.

Note the striking similarities between the track I found in Rickett's Glen and this one, which was found in Western PA. They are nearly identical.

Three-toed Bigfoot tracks are not uncommon in Pennsylvania, although they are less common then five-toed tracks. Researchers Stan Gordon and Eric Altman have both investigated cases where three-toed tracks were discovered in connection with a sighting of a Bigfoot creature. Stan Gordon made available to me a plaster cast of his three-toed track (fig. 4). Most striking is that the Gordon Track is nearly identical to the one I found in Rickett's Glen, having three toes and a curved heel.

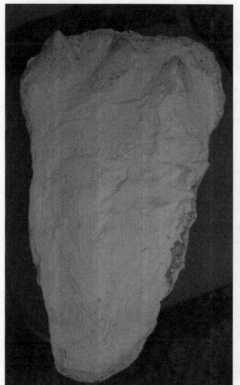 

Figure 5a. Three toed track from Pennsylvania given to Eric Altman. Probably found near Latrobe, PA.

Figure 5b. Three toed track from Eaton, Ohio. *Courtesy George Clappison, Ohio Bigfoot Research And Study Group*

When comparing the tracks side by side, it appears that the Gordon Track is slightly wider, but this may be due to the strata in which the track was made. Remember, a footprint is not necessarily the shape of the foot, but instead a record of the imprint the foot made in the ground. If the Gordon Track was made in thick mud, then the foot that made it probably slid around a bit before being withdrawn. The Altman Track (fig. 5a) was given to Eric by an individual who found it near Latrobe, PA and claimed that it came from a "12 foot tall violent beast that had a snout of a bear and tusks protruding from the snout … very violent and destructive." The elderly owner of the cast was known for embellishing his stories, but there is no evidence that he fabricated the cast completely. Using the Internet, I was able to locate a similar track which was found by a man near Eaton, Ohio (fig. 5b). Latrobe, it should be noted, is not too far away from the Pennsylvania/Ohio border. When compared side by side, the two tracks are nearly identical, however, they are very different from the tracks that Stan and I discovered.

Both the Altman and Ohio Tracks have three toes which terminate with claws. This, of course, is immediately suspicious because Bigfoot tracks have never shown signs of claw marks anywhere on them. When a researcher stumbles upon a track with five toes and claws, it usually turns out to be a bear print. In this case, however, we have to consider that both prints have three distinct toes, so they are unlikely the result of a bear. The two tracks also are wider and longer that the other three-toed tracks I have seen from elsewhere in Pennsylvania, indicating that perhaps the same creature made both the Altman and Ohio Tracks; however, it is unlikely that it was a Bigfoot.

There is the possibility that the three-toed tracks found in Pennsylvania and Ohio are the result of something entirely outside the Bigfoot phenomena. For many years, dating back to the legends of the Native American tribes, there have been stories and myths of giant birds known as Thunderbirds. These birds are said to be larger than condors, and have been reported to pick up animals, and sometimes even people! A bird's foot is uniquely shaped with four toes: three in the front, and one in the back, or, in some species, to the side. If a giant Thunderbird is still flying around, then it would naturally have to land occasionally to acquire food and would therefore leave giant footprints in its wake. Pennsylvania, incidentally, has the highest number of Thunderbird sightings in the nation. In 2005, I submitted a photo of the three-toed Rickett's Glen track to the producers of the *Coast to Coast AM* radio show with the suggestion that it might belong to a Thunderbird. This idea was met with considerable hostility after it was posted to the show's website. Everyone was sure it belonged to a Bigfoot, and refused to entertain any other possibility. What wonderful mainstream scientists they'll make someday.

There are also plenty of five-toed tracks found in Pennsylvania every year. I was fortunate enough to stumble upon a set of five-toed tracks while hiking once again through the woods of Rickett's Glen. On this occasion, I was in a remote part of the park that few hikers bother to visit. I came upon a dirt forest service road that was muddy as a result of heavy rains the night before. There, in the mud, was a clear Bigfoot track. This track was about ten inches long and six inches wide, which puts it in the category of a small Bigfoot track (a slight contradiction, I know). Based solely on its size, I would presume that it came from a young Bigfoot.

The track I discovered was only one in a line of eight footprints through the mud. The spacing of the footprints suggests that these were made by a bear; however, upon close inspection one can see that there are clearly no claw marks present in any of the tracks. This line of tracks continued for only a few feet, and terminated when the dirt road became too rocky for proper track-making.

These dramatic differences in the shape of the foot, and the reported difference in appearance of the creatures points to my emerging theory that there are different races, or even different species of Bigfoot creatures. The hypothetical races are best broken into three distinct groups. The Sasquatch, the Skunk Ape, and the Yeti; however, despite their differences, it is reasonable to say that all three are closely related.

Their distinguishing features are:

- Sasquatch has five toes, dark hair, and inhabits primarily the Pacific Northwest.
- Skunk Ape has three toes and lighter hair, and inhabits primarily the Southeast U.S.
- Yeti has five toes and white to gray hair and inhabits the Himalayan Mountain range.

I would like to stress that I believe we can use the blanket term "Bigfoot" for all of these creatures, we don't have to break them down into separate groups. It's just helpful to realize that when you find a three-toed footprint, it's not necessarily a completely different creature, more than likely, it's just a Skunk Ape.

PENNSYLVANIA INVESTIGATIONS

The first case I investigated was in the small town of Benton, Pennsylvania. One night, a woman was home alone while her husband was away on business, and before going to bed, she took her dog outside to go to the bathroom. While waiting for the dog to finish its business, the woman heard a terrible noise, which she described as a cross between a bear growling and a wolf howling. This horrible scream seemed to come from the forested hills and resonated through the valley where she lived. All the neighborhood dogs responded to this sound with uncontrollable barking. The howling and the dogs barking made her slightly uneasy, so she decided to go back into the house and wait there for her dog to finish.

A few moments after the woman was inside, she heard the terrible howling again, and then there was a loud crash at her front door. Opening the door to the front porch, she was shocked to see that her dog had jumped through the screen door, in an attempt to get inside. Whatever was howling in the woods scared her dog so badly that it couldn't stay outside any longer. This is a somewhat common reaction from dogs when in the presence of a Bigfoot creature, which leads me to believe that it was in fact a Bigfoot that was making those sounds.

A close friend and fellow paranormal colleague, George Morin, recently retold his story of a brief encounter with a Bigfoot creature. It was many years ago, when George was about ten years old. He recalls being at his grandparents' house near the town of Noxen, Pennsylvania. This area in the northern central region of the state is very rural and is surrounded by state game lands. George remembers walking outside by himself one blustery fall day, and stopping to look up at the trees. There, standing on a thick branch was what he described as a five foot tall monkey.

At the time, young George had no concept of Bigfoot, all he knew was that he saw what looked like a monkey up in the tree. He watched this creature, which was covered with dark brown hair, standing on the tree limb swaying back and forth as if it had nothing better to do. George ran inside to tell his parents what he had seen, and was met with little more than laughter, which is a normal response when a child tells you he is seeing "monkeys in the trees."

To this day, George is confident that he saw a young Bigfoot creature up in that tree behind his grandparents' house. The evidence that we have uncovered in our seven years of serious inquiry into the question of Bigfoot existing in Pennsylvania supports his sighting and his belief in what he saw. During an interview session in 1998, George's grandmother, Grace, told us that while she never actually saw a creature of any kind, sometimes during the summer she would smell a terrible sulfur smell coming from the woods behind her house. This sulfur smell is associated with the appearance of a

Bigfoot and usually indicates that one or more of the creatures is close by, even if they are not immediately visible to the eye.

We can only speculate as to the source of this foul-smelling odor. Dr. Grover Krantz suggested that it is the result of residual feces, sweat, and carrion that may be on the creature's fur. The combination of these scents, each repugnant on its own, can pack a powerful punch, as the same smell has been found on wild gorillas and naturalists note that the odor is prevalent for a hundred yards around the subject.

I had decided that there was a high probability that a Bigfoot creature was making its home somewhere in the area between the footprints I had found in Rickett's Glen and the sighting location near Noxen. After acquiring a detailed topographic map of the area, I determined that it was sufficiently remote for such a creature or small group of creatures to live there essentially undetected.

On the topographic map, there appeared to be a trail called "old railroad grade" running parallel to the creek through the entirety of the state game lands. It was my intention to find this trail and follow it through the woods, eventually terminating my journey at Noxen. While the area was remote, the trail turned out to be a forest service road that was open to public vehicles (a different service road then the aforementioned Bigfoot track was found on). Although the road was unimproved and really designed for a four-wheel-drive truck, I decided to take my little BMW on a back road excursion anyway.

The driving was going fine, and according to my map, I had two bridges to cross. The first was crossed with ease; however, the second one looked too unstable for my car to pass. So, I parked along the side of the road and headed out to follow the creek downstream as far as I could. It was a warm day, and with a small pack, I started into the woods that flanked both sides of the dirt road.

Only a few short yards from the road, I came upon a five-foot sapling with a piece of bark draped over one of its branches (fig. 6). This alone was not odd, but after careful inspection of the surrounding trees, I determined that the bark had come from a tree that was not in the immediate area. This indicated that it had been deliberately placed there by someone or something. It has been suggested that Bigfoot uses bark, rocks, and tree formations to mark its territory. Some have gone so far as to suggest that some bent tree formations are actually "Bigfoot artwork," although I would not hazard that approximation.

After studying the tree bark for several minutes, I made a note of it and continued onward through the brush. Approaching the creek, I was surprised to see that it was too high for me to cross safely. It's amazing how different the actual topography of this area was compared to the squiggly lines that were on the map I had used to plan this expedition. It was in my best interest to follow the creek bank instead of trying to cross at that point, so I kept walking, looking around the muddy ground for any sign of a footprint. Once I reached a point where I could no longer be certain of finding my way back to the car if it got dark, I decided to stop following the creek and cut through the woods to make it back to the forest service road.

Figure 6. Piece of bark draped over a tree limb. A possible Bigfoot territorial marker. Markers similar to this are frequently found in areas with high concentrations of Bigfoot sightings.

As I climbed a small embankment that led away from the creek, my eyes met an odd formation on the ground at the very top of the embankment. There was what looked like a narrow footprint in the dirt. It was no longer than eleven inches, and perhaps five inches wide but after some careful study, was unlikely a legitimate Bigfoot print.

Returning to the car, I decided to take one last look at the tree bark before heading home for the night. The bark was still there, draped carefully over the sapling tree branch. Cursing myself for not bringing a camera, I left the scene with the intention of returning to document the unusual marker.

It was December when I again visited the Rickett's Glen location, and on that occasion, I was more prepared to record any evidence that turned up. Although several months had passed since my last visit, I was delighted to find that the tree bark was still lying on the sapling tree branch. There was roughly a quarter inch of snow on the piece of bark, and probably three inches on the ground around the tree. If the bark had fallen off, which would've been likely in the heavy snow, then someone or something must have put it back where it was. This was one confirmation of my belief that a Bigfoot creature was using this bark as a territorial marker.

PROVING IT EXISTS/HUNTING THE CREATURE

To kill or not to kill, that is the question!

The majority of Bigfoot researchers today are taking a no-kill approach to their research, being content to record sightings, cast tracks, and plunge into the woods with cameras hoping to obtain photographic evidence of their quarry. While most are well-intentioned, it is an utterly hopeless way to pursue their goal. The Patterson Film is by far the most conclusive photographic proof of the creature, and there is no shortage of skeptics who simply refuse to believe that the creature in the film is real. Any further photographs or videos will probably not be as first-rate as the Patterson Film, and therefore will be useless except to impress fellow Bigfoot researchers. Stuart Chase said it best: "For those who believe, no proof is necessary. For those who don't believe, no proof is possible."

Many Bigfoot researchers spend an inordinate amount of time setting up and maintaining motion-sensing game cameras in remote areas where Bigfoot has been reported in the past. These cameras have never yielded sufficient photographic evidence to prove that such a creature exists. While the cameras are loaded with shots of deer, bear, and other wildlife, none have ever successfully captured the image of a Bigfoot. How can this be? I puzzled over this question for quite a while before being introduced to William Dranginis, founder of the Virginia Bigfoot Research Organization.

William (don't call him Bill) is the creator of the Bigfoot Primate Research Lab, a mobile van designed exclusively to document the existence of these creatures. The BPRL is packed to the hilt with technological gadgetry. He has night vision scopes, motion-activated cameras, sound recorders, numerous video cameras and the van itself is sporting a thermal video camera attached to a 24-foot mast, all of which is networked into a state of the art recording system. This stuff is very impressive and must truly be seen to be believed.

One of the most important things I learned from William was the concept of ultrasonic leaks. All electronic gadgets emit sound on the ultrasonic frequency. This is too low for human ears to hear, but through numerous unintentional field experiments, William determined that animals can detect sounds at this frequency. He purchased an ultrasonic leak detector, which converts the low pitch into an audible sound, and discovered that all of his game cameras were emitting a horrible squealing sound. Obviously, Bigfoot, like the other animals of the forest, is able to hear this, and is intelligent enough to stay away from the sound. This could also explain why researchers who hike into the woods with cameras hoping to film a Bigfoot usually come away disappointed.

Figure 7. An example of a possible territorial marker. This marker was found in the Great Dismal Swamp of Virginia where much of my field research has been conducted.

Fortunately, William has found a way to mask the ultrasonic leak that emanates from his cameras. It is my understanding that he is going to patent and mass market this pending innovation as a "Gotcha Cam" and therefore, I will refrain from giving away the details of his device. Although, I can say from personal experience that it is quite impressive.

When talking with William in 2004, he spent about an hour showing me and some fellow researchers all of his equipment, and after pausing for "oohs" and "ahhs" he admitted that in all his years of using all this stuff, he has only one blurry, inconclusive photo to show for it. He is now abandoning the techno-search and moving towards a shamanistic approach that includes such alternative sciences as remote viewing.

Another path to proving the existence of Bigfoot was developed by Robert W. Morgan of the American Anthropological Research Foundation. In his two audio books *The Bigfoot Pocket Field Manual* and *Bigfoot: The Ultimate Adventure*, Robert explains how he was able to approach these creatures using the Diane Fossey method of immersion in the creature's environment. Morgan spent five calculated years hiking into the woods, building the trust of the "Forest Giants" in the same way an anthropologist would build the trust of the apes they were studying.

He did this by having immeasurable patience and following a few simple rules. These were hiking alone, or in a very small group; never carrying a camera which might be perceived as a gun; always adopting a defensive posture when confronted with the strange sounds that a Bigfoot makes; and identifying himself by making a particular noise whenever he entered the Bigfoot territory. Over the course of five long years, Morgan was able to gain the trust of a group of Bigfoot creatures living in southeast Ohio. Don't be mistaken, they didn't come out and shake his hand or start talking with him, but when Morgan entered their territory, he would make a certain sound that he had made over and over and the creatures

Figure 8. The author rowing through the Great Dismal Swamp in pursuit of his elusive quarry.

knew he was not going to harm them and would come into view.

Morgan's plan was to bring several scientists into the field with him and then coax the creatures into appearing. If the group of scientists saw Bigfoot for themselves, he reasoned, then they could not deny its existence. On the eve of the conclusion of his project, one of his assistants decided to get drunk with some friends and hike into the woods with loaded guns. This assistant made the familiar "Morgan call" and when a Bigfoot appeared on the ridge of the mountain above them, all their guns started blazing. The creatures have not responded to Morgan's call since that night. This stupid prank cost Morgan five years of hard work, five years which he may never get back.

After corresponding with Robert Morgan over the course of several months and meeting with people in his organization, I have determined that his novel approach is probably our best bet to proving that a creature such as Bigfoot does exist. It is ideal because Morgan's method requires little funding due to the lack of equipment required. However, part of the difficulty in using Morgan's method is that it takes time and patience. Most serious Bigfoot researchers are currently employed full-time and are not able to devote the man-hours required for such a project, and therefore it is unlikely that expeditions of this kind will be undertaken by outside parties in the foreseeable future.

The antithesis of this is the method suggested by Dr. Grover Krantz whereby two people would drive down forest service roads in the middle of the night looking for Bigfoot with a high-power spot light and a rifle. He reasoned that a substantial number of Bigfoot sightings occur in roadside encounters, so this might be the best way to find and recover a specimen. The obvious danger of this is expressed by Dr. Krantz, and in his book he recalls once seeing an upright humanoid walking along the road that turned out to be a man wearing a dark sweatshirt, and he acknowledges that a less

34

experienced hunter might have taken a few overzealous shots before realizing that it was a man.

That warning aside, the problem of transporting the body of a Bigfoot, whether found naturally dead, or otherwise, is one that few researchers consider before heading out into the dense wilderness. If they leave the body to get help to bring it back to civilization, it is unlikely that the body will be there when they return. Carrying it back single-handedly would be impossible, unless Lou Ferrigno has recently taken up Bigfoot hunting as a hobby. Therefore, Krantz's method of roadside hunting might be the only way to successfully bring an entire body back to civilization where it can be studied by scientists. However, because of the inherent danger of misidentification, this author strongly recommends against it.

CONCLUSION

I should not close this chapter without mentioning my own qualifications for claiming to be a Bigfoot expert. Unlike most researchers, I actually took the time to study anthropology at my university, although this was not my first choice at that particular institution. When I was a senior in high school, I was also a freshman in college at Bloomsburg University. I had been accepted into their theater program a year early due to my ability as an actor, and it was in that capacity that I had intended to make my name in the world.

After two years of hard work, I had taken nearly all the undergraduate acting classes at BU, so, in an effort to learn more about the scientific principles of Bigfoot, I decided to take a look at the courses offered by the anthropology department. I wanted to meet all the professors personally to see if there were any who might be actively engaged in studying the Bigfoot question and my interviews were surprising to say the least.

The first person I encountered was Dr. Wymer, an archaeologist who actually developed a course of instruction called "Pseudoscience" in which she goes about debunking "myths" such as psychic phenomena, UFOs, and of course, Bigfoot. Our first meeting was in the anthropology lab, and I told her very directly that I believe in Bigfoot and this belief was fueling my interest in anthropology. Her response bordered on hysteria. She began ranting and raving, telling me that Bigfoot is just a myth and Grover Krantz (yes, she mentioned him by name) is just "a kook mythology professor who doesn't know the difference between reality and a myth."

I then calmly explained to her that I was going to find Bigfoot someday and prove that it existed and that I would be on the cover of *National Geographic*. Dr. Wymer responded with another diatribe saying: "You go for it. I've already been there! You go for it!" I assured her that I would, and then promptly left. Somehow, she was successful in preventing me from ever taking her Pseudoscience class, although some friends of mine who were in the class told me that she would frequently make an example of me as if I were a professional colleague with whom she disagreed.

That unpleasantness aside, I did continue as a dual theater/anthropology major for my last two years at Bloomsburg University. Among my more considerable achievements was a literature review for a cultural anthropology class in which I advocated the serious scientific study of Sasquatch, and also persuaded some of my professors to admit that there might be more to Bigfoot than their colleagues suggested.

Bigfoot, I acknowledge, is not the most important thing in the world. There are starving children, homeless veterans, and genocidal crises in Africa that we need to worry about. No one should blame serious scientists for not giving Bigfoot their top priority; they do actually have other things to focus their time and money on. However, if we realize that the creature will never be found by anyone other than dedicated researchers, then we can begin to work together and someday make that "big find."

CHAPTER 2

UFOs and Aliens

UFOs, Unidentified Flying Objects, are unquestionably real. It is a fact that people occasionally see things flying through the sky that they cannot identify. It is also true however that the vast majority of UFOs do have relatively mundane explanations. I can remember one encounter with a UFO early in the morning, while driving a friend home from a party. We diverted our course to follow the object through the sky. Finding ourselves perplexed after a few minutes, we parked the car on top of a hill and got out to study it. After roughly twenty minutes of careful observation, we determined that the UFO was nothing more than the planet Venus. Slightly discouraged, we got back into our car and decided to never repeat that action unless we were absolutely sure the object was actually moving.

The term Flying Saucer is more widely used to indicate that the object in the sky is of extraterrestrial origin, or can be identified as a previously unknown form of flying craft. Most UFO researchers are more comfortable describing their quarry as a Flying Saucer, rather than the ubiquitous UFO. I have chosen to use both terms interchangeably throughout this chapter, although when Flying Saucer is used, it is always in connection with some kind of mysterious flying craft, not just a light in the sky.

The UFO and alien abduction phenomenon is unique among paranormal subjects in that there is nothing an investigator can do to conclusively prove they exist. There are numerous pictures of UFOs and Flying Saucers, yet we cannot say for certain where they come from or what they are doing. Thousands of abductees have come forward with their stories about painful medical experiments performed by seemingly alien creatures, but it is not possible for us to grab one of these creatures and throw it on the White House lawn the way we could with Bigfoot.

Alas, UFO researchers must be content to catalogue sighting events and record the stories of abductees while watching the night sky hoping for a sign of contact which can be photographed as further proof that something is indeed out there. In the following chapter, I will attempt to explain the hows and whys of the UFO phenomena using two specific cases as examples to suffice for UFO cases at large.

PINE BUSH, NEW YORK

The hamlet of Pine Bush is located in the Hudson Valley in the southeast corner of New York, roughly seventy miles north of the Big Apple. The Hudson Valley is a fairly rural area that has been a hotbed of UFO sightings for the last thirty years. Two books have been written about the Pine Bush Phenomena, as it is now referred to by authors and UFO buffs. The first was *Night Siege* in 1987 by Phil Imbrogno, and the second, *Silent Invasion* in 1991 by Dr. Ellen Crystal, was responsible for the influx of sky watchers pouring into Pine Bush hoping to catch a glimpse of the UFOs described in her book, although it was considered by some UFOlogists to be the product of outright fantasy.

The Pine Bush Phenomena goes beyond just typical UFO sightings. It is possible to see UFOs in the vicinity of Pine

Figure 10. Valley to the north of Pine Bush. Photograph was taken from the hilltop where I had my UFO sighting. It's a perfect viewing area, and the scenery is spectacular.

Bush on almost any given night, but the physical appearance of the craft and their accompanying lights are not always consistent from sighting to sighting. For example, one night while I was sitting out on the overlook (fig. 10) that is about one mile north of Pine Bush proper on Route 52, a friend and I witnessed two different UFOs on two separate occasions performing aerial maneuvers in the sky.

Our sightings occurred in March of 2000. Shortly after parking on the hill at 11:30 p.m., my friend Jean pointed out a bright, full light in the middle of the sky, well above the horizon. There was no moon that night, but what we saw was as big as the moon. The brightness of the object can only be compared to a headlight at close range, yet the light was completely contained, so it was definitely not a spot light. The light appeared, hovered in one spot for a matter of seconds and then disappeared.

We both stood there, amazed, doing a reality check just to make sure we both had witnessed the same thing, not knowing that we only had to wait a few more minutes for our next sighting. In the same area of the sky, about five minutes later, we saw what appeared to be a small white light performing impossible aerial maneuvers. It flew in an irregular triangular pattern for a matter of seconds and then flashed once before disappearing completely. The two objects that we saw were clearly different in appearance and behavior, yet one is inclined to believe that they are the result of the same phenomena. It is important to note that Pine Bush Phenomena expert Dr. Bruce Cornet determined that the majority of UFO sightings in the Hudson Valley occur between the hours of 7 p.m. and midnight, making our sighting typical.

Other visitors to Pine Bush have reported seeing large triangular and boomerang shaped craft. These craft are usually reported to be in excess of 500 feet in diameter and sometimes larger. There are numerous pictures of these UFOs available over the Internet and in the above-mentioned books. Probably the most significant event in Pine Bush UFOlogy was the Hudson Valley Mass Sighting.

On August 6th, 1992 at approximately 9:43 p.m., hundreds of people witnessed a large boomerang-shaped craft flying at low altitude over the Hudson Valley. Police stations were inundated with phone calls from concerned citizens who were frightened by the appearance of the otherworldly craft. This sighting was well-documented by UFO researchers and stands as one of the most convincing sighting events in the history of UFOlogy.

One of the more interesting aspects of the Pine Bush UFO sightings is the alleged ghostly apparitions which are occasionally encountered in the same areas where UFOs are normally spotted. Some local researchers have photographs of orb phenomena, which are commonly associated with ghosts, appearing in conjunction with UFOs. In an interview with local paranormal investigator Roger in 1999, he stated that he has numerous pictures of orbs taken all around Pine Bush, and curiously, a picture of a "ghostly old man who resembles a Grey alien."

During our first interview, Roger told me a story about the United States Army killing a commune of Native Americans in the late 1800s on the outskirts of Pine Bush. He suggested that this massacre is somehow connected with the ghost activity and partially connected to the strange lights that are seen in the skies. Although he is not prepared to say that one is the result of the other, Roger still believes that the UFOs may be of extraterrestrial origin. I have been unable to find any solid evidence that such a massacre ever occurred, although Roger and I never made a trip to the site where this supposedly happened. One can presume that a proper excavation of the massacre location would yield enough evidence to prove that it did or did not occur.

Doctor Bruce Cornet, whose professional background is in geology, has numerous photographs of UFOs flying over Pine Bush. Some of these are truly amazing and several show the craft making a ninety-degree dive straight down to the ground and then disappearing from view. This, coupled with the magnetic anomalies that Dr. Cornet has discovered and recorded, suggest to him that the UFOs are somehow hiding beneath the surface of the earth. He acknowledges that this sounds a bit fantastic, but the evidence he has collected points to this possibility.

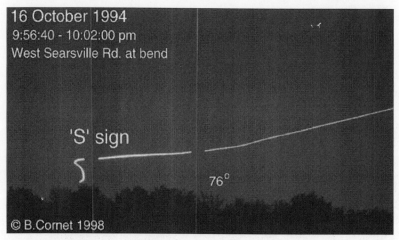

Figure 10. Light trail photographed by Dr. Bruce Cornet at night in the sky over Pine Bush, NY. *Courtesy of B. Cornet*

Figure 11. The author in front of Butch Hunt's barber shop in Pine Bush in 1999.

While taking magnetic readings along Albany Post Road in June 1992, Dr. Cornet had a close encounter of his own. Standing next to a large field with his instruments running, he suddenly heard a "shot" and felt a sharp sting in his chest. When this occurred, he could see his shirt move in and out where the "shot" supposedly hit him which left a round bruise the size of a quarter on his lower chest. The x-rays of his chest taken immediately after showed no irregular materials in his body. In addition to this experience, Dr. Cornet has had numerous abduction experiences while in Pine Bush.

My own investigation into the Pine Bush Phenomena yielded little more than an exhilarating UFO sighting and interesting stories from Roger, as well as one other gem of the Hudson Valley. Butch Hunt owns a little barber shop on the main street of town and is good for an inexpensive haircut and UFO talk whenever you're in town. I highly recommend visiting his shop, even if your follicles are challenged; it's a veritable roadside museum of UFO memorabilia. If you're interested, just look for the barber pole, you'll find it right next to the drawing of a green alien that sits in the window of Butch's shop.

It is my belief that the Pine Bush Phenomena should continue to be documented and recorded by serious, dedicated researchers. The high number of UFO sightings from credible witnesses in addition to the sound scientific data gathered by Dr. Bruce Cornet and others suggests that something very real is visiting the Hudson Valley from above.

THE KECKSBURG UFO CRASH

In December of 1965, something happened in Kecksburg, Pennsylvania that would change the lives of its residents forever. On December 9th, shortly before 5 p.m., a fireball crashed in the woods just east of Kecksburg. Eyewitness accounts claim the military showed up and closed the site, but others say there was no government presence at all. Some believe the fireball was a UFO, others think it was a Soviet satellite, while the rest are sure it was only a meteor. Whatever it was, *something* crashed in those woods that night in 1965.

When I arrived in Kecksburg for the first time in 1999, I entered the local fire hall, which is the "hang out" for the hamlet's tiny population. My assistant and I established contact with two men there, Barney and Ray, both of whom were firemen. Barney said nothing during the entire interview; however, Ray was there on the night of the crash and happens to be friends with the landowner in whose woods the object crashed. I asked him about the presence of military personnel, and he said he saw some Navy jeeps but no big trucks. An important factor that had not been previously mentioned by any researcher is the fact that it was hunting season when the crash happened and all the hunters were in the woods the next day, poking around to see what had occurred there the night before.

Ray confirmed that if there had been big trucks, they couldn't have gotten down into the woods because of a steep hill or ravine. He also said that on the night of the crash, there were "a good hundred people" walking around the site, and the only thing preventing public access was the line of cars parked along the side of the road. Ray didn't believe that what crashed was a UFO, which he consistently referred to as a "sputnik."

The Kecksburg fireball occurred during the annual Geminid meteor shower when over fifty meteors strike the Earth's atmosphere every hour. A similar fireball was reported in California not long after the Kecksburg event. In addition to the timing, the fireball was first seen in Canada and then by witnesses from Michigan, Indiana and Ohio before finally crashing in the woods of Pennsylvania. Pieces of the fireball were strewn throughout these states, and baseball-sized hunks of flaming metal were recovered — not by the military, but by children who had been out playing that night.

Figure 12. Barney, the author, and Ray in the Kecksburg Fire Hall in 1999.

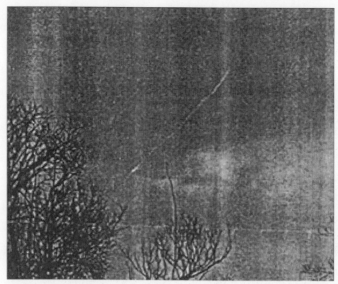

Figure 13. Photograph of the fireball train of December 9, 1965, taken by Lowell Wright in Michigan.

Astronomer Von Del Chamberlain, who was working at Michigan State University when the fireball appeared and later became director of the Hansen Planetarium, plotted the object's track and its speed. He determined, using photographs and eyewitness reports, that the fireball was moving at nearly nine miles per second, which is much too fast for a man-made craft entering the Earth's atmosphere. "It was clearly a meteorite event ... It's also a very typical event in many ways. The fireball, the trail that was left in the sky afterward, the sonic booms. And the confusion that results is also typical," Chamberlain said.

The material dropping from the fireball caused numerous small fires along its path of descent. Ed Myers was the Kecksburg fire chief in December 1965, and his cousin Jim Mayes was the assistant fire chief. Shortly after the incident, Mayes talked to the press and said he had escorted a few military men from a nearby base, but they didn't find anything. Major Hector Quintanilla, the man in charge of the Wright-Patterson AFB office of UFO investigation said a team had been dispatched from the Pittsburg area to investigate the crash. While conducting this research, I wondered if any of my co-workers might have additional information to add concerning military investigation of unusual weather events, such as meteors.

I asked a Navy Aerographer's Mate (meteorologist) if there was any possibility of shore-based personnel investigating a meteorite crash. "They would be interested, certainly. There also might be some cooperation with civilian weather agencies," he said. This is particularly significant because both Stan Gordon and I have collected separate eyewitness reports which suggest that Navy personnel were involved in the crash investigation and the recovery that supposedly followed.

Many researchers have suggested that the Kecksburg object was actually of Soviet origin. The propagation of this theory has been aided by a few unusual or coincidental factors. Firstly, on the same day, fourteen hours earlier, a Soviet Space probe named Kosmos 96 failed en route to Venus and crashed in Canada. Also, one of the alleged eyewitnesses of the Kecksburg UFO claimed that the object had writing like "Egyptian hieroglyphics" on it, which could have been confused with Russian characters, although one witness has a strong Russian background and likely would have recognized such text.

A crashed Russian satellite or piece of a Soviet missile would explain the military's desire to recover the debris and maintain a cover of secrecy concerning the event. Chamberlain's report stresses that the trajectory and speed of the object were simply not consistent with man-made materials entering the atmosphere. The theory that the object was of Soviet origin is mostly based upon the Kosmos 96 crash, and while the satellite definitely landed in Canada, there has been speculation that perhaps a piece of it came down in Kecksburg. However, it is highly unlikely that two parts of the same object would've entered the atmosphere fourteen hours apart from one another. Besides, NATO returned what was left of Kosmos 96

Figure 14. A model of the Kosmos space probe.

to the Soviet government, so why wouldn't they follow the
same protocol if the Kecksburg object was a part of the same
satellite?

If we eliminate the possibility of a meteor or a Soviet
probe, we are left with something unknown. Some local
citizens of Kecksburg claim that the object was not from this
planet and that the government recovered this alien craft. In
1990, the TV show *Unsolved Mysteries* ran a documentary
piece on the Kecksburg incident. Former Fire Chief Ed Myers
believes that people got so carried away that they started
making up stories, hoping to get on television. "In reality, there

were two or three military men, but the number kept growing as the tale was told and retold," he said in a recent interview.

Astronomer Robert Young contends that some of the alleged eyewitnesses decided to just flat out lie to reporters and investigators. One alleged witness was later found to have been in prison on the night of the crash, another falsely claimed to be the Kecksburg fire chief, and yet another witness has threatened legal action against any resident that would make statements contradicting him on national television. According to Young, the eyewitness accounts make up the bulk of the evidence supporting a UFO crash and retrieval, and he further contends that these eyewitnesses have a history of unreliable testimony.

Kecksburg expert Stan Gordon has based much of his argument for the unearthly origin of the object on eyewitness accounts he's collected over the past few decades. James Romansky gave Stan a detailed description of the crashed object and said that it seemed to have been "liquid metal poured into a mold" and that it had "no seams." James also said that he saw writing, like hieroglyphics, on the outer rim of the craft. Some sources say the military showed up, cordoned off the crash site and took the object to Wright-Patterson Air Force Base where it was further studied by personnel from the U.S. Navy. There has even been some talk that a body (human or alien?) was recovered, but Stan is cautious: "We have no way to prove that."

One man that Stan interviewed said that he saw a military jet pursuing the object as it slowly descended to the Earth. If this is true, then it's possible the government was aware of the object's existence before it entered the atmosphere. This might help explain how the military agents said to be at the scene arrived so quickly. They were prepared ahead of time.

Robert Young's 1996 report titled *The Investigation of the Kecksburg UFO Crash* was graciously given to me by Robert when I was a budding seventeen-year-old UFO researcher. The report is very interesting, and is a refreshingly contradictory view of Stan Gordon's analysis of the events of

1965. Young has amassed an impressive 200 eyewitness accounts, and he claims that only ten of them are even close to supporting Gordon's crash and retrieval story. He then successfully tears apart each eyewitness's testimony, and appears to have contacted a great number of them in an attempt to verify their stories. However, there are a few loopholes that Young leaves in his statements, which cannot be addressed using the evidence that he has collected.

The Investigation of the Kecksburg UFO Crash goes so far as to state: "The object was a meteor which never came near Pennsylvania." If this is true, then what did all those eyewitnesses see in the sky over Pennsylvania that night, and what crashed in the woods? Is it possible that two different objects entered the earth's atmosphere at the same time? Perhaps the Ontario Fireball was only a part of the spacecraft that crashed in the woods outside Kecksburg. Of course, based on Chamberlain's calculations, whatever the object was, it was not man-made, and therefore must be of extraterrestrial origin. Stan Gordon has collected physical evidence that shows burn damage on the tree tops at the crash site and the damage has been dated to 1965. This is something Robert Young failed to address in his report, probably because it proves conclusively that something crashed in Kecksburg.

One of the eyewitnesses interviewed by Stan Gordon claimed to have been at Wright-Patterson Air Force Base on the night of the Kecksburg crash, and stated that he saw the recovered UFO in a hangar. Some of the personnel he interviewed claimed to have seen Navy technicians, who were either working on or guarding the craft. One inconsistency in his story is that the Navy personnel were wearing command ball caps. For many years, sailors wore black or white "dixie cups" as head gear, but this was changed during the Vietnam War, and all sailors were given baseball caps that have the name of their command embroidered on the front, a practice that is still in place to this day. However, the shift to ball caps occurred after

1965, so therefore, this particular story should be taken with a grain of salt.

The December 10th newspaper story run by *The Press Enterprise* stated that Michigan Sheriff Deputies were dispatched to investigate reports that an object crashed south of Lapeer. Sheriff Kenneth Parks was responsible for the investigation and reported to the media that his deputies "found nothing except a 'couple handfuls' of shiny metallic foil, each piece about 4 - 6 inches long and about a quarter-inch wide." *Found nothing?* This extremely important factor was tucked on the second page, towards the end of the article, and yet, it is one of the most significant aspects of the case!

If the deputies found metallic foil at a crash site in Michigan, then obviously there were two separate objects in the earth's atmosphere that night. One which was reported as the Ontario Fireball must have crashed in Michigan, and the second blazed through Ohio and plummeted into Kecksburg. I am not an expert on meteorites, by any means, but I am fairly confident that they are not made of shiny metallic foil. Another alarming factor is that identical material was reported at the scene of the Roswell, New Mexico crash, which suggests that both incidents involved similar craft. Sheriff Kenneth Parks passed away in 2003, and my correspondence to his son was left unanswered.

Some think this is a model case that demonstrates how the government conceals UFO information. Conclusive proof, beyond eyewitness testimony, will be difficult to find. The man who owns the property where the fireball allegedly crashed does not welcome investigators, and wants nothing to do with the media. Neither the Kecksburg nor Michigan crash sites have been excavated, although if done properly, the entire issue might be laid to rest once and for all.

THE GREYS AND THEIR AGENDA

UFOlogist Stanton Friedman once publicly asked the question: why do the Greys take the time to put us back in our

50

beds and wipe out our memories? This is probably the most profound question that has ever been asked about the alien abduction phenomenon, and yet very few researchers have taken the time to try to answer it. That question got me thinking, and I remembered an article that was in *Popular Science* in the 1988-89 time period (I have been unable to find the article again) which attempted to predict what a human being might look like 100,000 years from now.

Their description was put simply and directly. Future humans would be small, to accommodate the pressure of an increased population. They would be thin and have very little muscle mass due to increasing reliance on hundreds of years of automation to do all the heavy lifting work for them. In the future, humans will have very large brains and very large eyes

Figure 15. *The meeting of a lifetime…* The author meets with noted nuclear physicist and UFOlogist Stanton Friedman in Pennsylvania in 2003. Mr. Friedman is a leading proponent in the effort to uncover the government's hidden agenda concerning UFOs.

which are well suited to staring into a computer screen for hours and hours (we're already doing this today). All vestigial organs will be eliminated, no hair, no nails, no lips, no external ears. Skin color will no longer be a discriminating factor in future human beings because centuries of interracial breeding will leave the entire species with a pasty gray skin tone. Although the article's description of a future human was meaningless to me at the time, it would be another year before I would read *Creatures From UFOs* by Daniel Cohen and first begin to piece together the mystery behind the Grey Aliens.

Allow me to preface the following paragraphs with this statement. I do believe in the possibility of life on other planets (intelligent and otherwise). And I also believe that some of these alien civilizations may have visited the earth and perhaps may even abduct people from time to time. However, the theory I have developed suggests that the Greys are not aliens from another planet, but are actually human beings from the distant future who are traveling through time to fulfill their agenda of preservation of the species.

The most commonly sighted alien being is the humanoid Grey which can be accurately described using the same terms in the above description of the future human beings. The first known modern day encounter with the Greys occurred on September 19th, 1941 in the White Mountains of New Hampshire. Betty and Barney Hill are the most famous alien abductees because they were the first to publicly report their experience.

The Hills were driving down Route 3 when they noticed a strange white light in the sky that seemed to be following them. Eventually, they stopped the car and Barney got out to look at the object. Using binoculars, he was able to see the flying saucer clearly and could see beings standing against a large window in front of the craft. He would later draw a picture of these spacemen, and so the modern concept of Grey aliens was born.

Both husband and wife would later undergo hypnotic regression therapy to recall what happened to them after their initial encounter with the strange flying disk. They said that the Greys had taken them into the flying saucer and conducted intrusive medical experiments on them, taking semen from Barney and inserting a large needle into Betty's abdomen. Betty was able to recall that the Greys took her on a brief tour of their ship and even showed her a star map, explaining that they were from another planet. This star map has been recreated and is thought to represent the Zeta Reticuli system.

It seems highly unusual that the Greys would tell Betty something as important as their home planet, and then wipe out her memory so she could never tell anyone; they obviously gave her that information for a reason. I believe that it was deliberate disinformation designed to mislead not only the Hills, but every alien abductee. This begs the question: Why bother to deceive at all? Why don't the Greys just tell us why they're really here and maybe we can work together? The answer is found in the physics of time travel.

The Grandfather Paradox suggests that if you traveled back in time and killed your own grandfather, you would cease to exist because you would never have been born. In the same vein, minor changes that are made in the past could have an unpredictable outcome on the course of world events in the future. This is one of the fundamental problems with the physics of time travel, and one reason why some physicists and philosophers feel that time travel is impossible.

This explains perfectly why the Greys erase from the abductee's mind the memory of their abduction experience and why every abductee is placed back in their beds after two or three hours of medical procedures. The Greys do not want to upset the space/time continuum thereby altering their own future reality and therefore they take all necessary precautions to ensure their victims have no memory of the experience. As a safeguard, the idea that the Greys are a member of some distant race of aliens is suggested to further confuse the abductee and discourage the abductee from speaking out about their experience.

Another issue with the Grey's supposed alien identity was raised in H.G. Wells' *War of the Worlds*. Any alien species would not have a natural immunity to our earthly viruses and we would not have any immunity to theirs. The aliens would quickly become infected through contact with humans and they would not last very long on our planet. Likewise, humans who were abducted would be exposed to diseases that the aliens didn't even know they were carrying. The European invaders spread disease among native populations when they came into contact with the Amerindians, causing hundreds of thousands of deaths. By the same token, Europeans found their ranks decimated by native scourges such as malaria.

Humans traveling from the future would not have to worry about contracting diseases to which they were already genetically immune. They would, however, have to take precautions when interacting with abductees because their futuristic diseases would be easily transmitted to us. Perhaps they are immunizing the abductees on their first contact experience.

So, why are future humans traveling back in time to perform medical procedures on their present day ancestors? All of the procedures seem to focus on the reproductive system and there are numerous accounts of female abductees being impregnated and then having a miscarriage after an abduction experience. Some abductees have even reported seeing large incubation rooms filled with hybrid human/Grey fetuses aboard the flying saucer. We can find the answer to our question by analyzing the physical description of the Greys that abductees have provided. Nearly every single abductee has stated that the Greys have no visible reproductive organs. This is the most significant part of their anatomy, and yet it is rarely commented on by alien abduction researchers.

Truly, we can only speculate as to why the Greys have no genitalia, but it is my assertion that due to sexually

54

transmitted diseases, and ease of genetic modification, future humans completely abstain from sexual intercourse. All conception takes place in a laboratory environment and eventually humans cease to have reproductive organs at all. Perhaps somewhere along the line their genetic stock became contaminated or some catastrophe befell the laboratory where these procedures take place. Whatever the case, the Greys were forced to return to a time in their past (our present) to acquire uncorrupted DNA from a species similar to their own. This would also explain why some people are abducted again and again, and why their children are sometimes abducted as well. It is probable that the Greys would've worked out which bloodlines had qualities desirable to the future human race, and are only sampling from those groups. One way to prove this theory is for us to take DNA sampling of every abductee and then compare their genetic makeup to determine if there is a pattern. Of course, a very large group of abductees would have to participate in the study to reduce the number of potentially fraudulent cases that would undoubtedly be present.

Even if aliens from another planet are visiting earth, their flying saucers must have the ability to warp or bend the time/space continuum somehow in order to travel such long distances. The theory that Greys are using principles of time travel to get from one place to another has already been considered by several authors on the subject of UFOs. However, no one has bothered to reason that if they can travel through time, they do not necessarily have to be coming from another planet.

If we pull back the mists of antiquity and look at ancient and historical encounters with aliens, we will see that time-traveling Greys can account for UFO sightings all throughout human history. Why would they bother to go so far back in time? Imagine if we had the ability to travel through time today. Wouldn't historians have the most to gain from such a technology? Civil War buffs would be standing in line to get a glimpse of the Battle of Gettysburg and Egyptologists could marvel while watching the construction of the pyramids. Basic human curiosity about where we are from has motivated the Greys to canvas history, searching to further their knowledge of the human race.

I have already stated that I believe the Greys are the greatest perpetrators of the belief that flying saucers and their occupants are alien in nature, but what about the government? UFO buffs and conspiracy theorists are confident that the governments of the world are hiding information from the public about UFOs and orchestrating cover-ups whenever one crashes. However, another question that is rarely asked is: Why? Why would the United States government (or any foreign equivalent) want to conceal the existence of extraterrestrial life?

Let's go back to the UFO crash at Roswell, New Mexico and work forward from there. Pilot Kenneth Arnold first reported seeing "Flying Saucers" while flying his personal small plane over Mount Rainier. This story was widely circulated in the news and Kenneth Arnold became the first modern day eyewitness of a Flying Saucer. About two weeks later, one of these Saucers crashed outside of Roswell, New Mexico in July 1947. The time periods of these events are so close, that one cannot help but think they are the result of the same phenomena.

After the crash, military units from the Army-Air Force arrived and secured the scene, taking away all the wreckage and silencing any witnesses who happened to be in the area at the time. The eyewitness stories are some of the most compelling in the history of UFOlogy. Some people claim to have seen alien bodies near the crashed Saucer, one of which was still alive when the military personnel arrived. The description of these bodies perfectly matches those of the Greys.

Why would the government not want the American people to know what crashed at Roswell? At first, they did want us to know. The press release from the U.S. military on July 8th stated that a flying saucer had been recovered and then transferred to "higher headquarters," presumably for further study. Very shortly after the news was released, Brigadier General Roger Ramey came back and changed the story, saying that what had been found was nothing more than a weather balloon. At the time, that was enough to shut the media up, but in reality, it is highly unlikely that an Army-Air Force Intelligence Officer would have mistaken a weather balloon for a flying saucer.

Far more likely is that the Army-Air Force recovered the crashed Saucer and the occupants. And when the survivor of the craft explained to the military agents what they were and where they came from, they convinced the government to not breathe a word of their project to the American public for fear of disrupting the time/space continuum and creating a massive Grandfather Paradox effect. This is why the government has a vested interest in protecting the American people from what they don't already know and reinforcing the belief that UFOs and flying saucers are of an extraterrestrial origin with smoke screen tactics such as Project Blue Book. By helping the Greys conceal their activities, the U.S. government is helping the human race as a whole; true, it's a human race that's potentially hundreds of thousands of years in the future, but the human race, no less.

I mean, honestly, if the Greys were truly aliens from another planet with sinister intentions towards the human race then why would the U.S. government, or any human being for that matter, help them keep their evil plans a secret? And why, if their agenda is so diabolically covert, would magnets, stickers, and coffee mugs with the Grey's bug-eyed visage be hawked like garage sale trinkets? All of this is actually helping the Greys convince us that they are aliens and that a thin, large-headed, big-eyed humanoid is exactly what aliens from another planet are supposed to look like. So if we see one, or are ever abducted by a group of them, we *know for sure* that what happened to us was an "alien abduction."

So, if this is true, then why don't the Greys shut me up and prevent this book from being published? Who knows, maybe my great-grandson invents a prototype of a time machine and killing me would create a Great-Grandfather Paradox. You get the picture. I actually did try, on two separate occasions, to release this theory to the public, but both times, it seemed to go nowhere. In 1998 I mailed an unsolicited, handwritten note containing the basics of my theory to eight prominent UFO researchers. None of them ever acted on or repeated the information, so I presume that they simply found it preposterous.

Considering the evidence supporting my theory of time-traveling Greys, I would like to christen them *Homo futurus*, although perhaps this designation should be withheld pending biological proof of their existence.

The final question we have to ask is what can we do about this situation? As I see it, there are two avenues of approach, both equally unattractive. We can sit back and allow the Greys to continue their fertilization project unfettered (as we are basically already doing), content with the knowledge that what they are doing is serving the greater good of humanity and their intrusive medical procedures will ensure that the human race truly never dies out. Or, an ambitious researcher could continue hounding the government, demanding to see top secret documents and recording the stories of abductees, perhaps even developing the aforementioned DNA database, hoping that eventually with enough evidence they might be able to meet the Greys face to face and say "Stop this. What you're doing is not right. If the human race is going to die out, just let it."

This author has not yet decided which course of action to take, but I'll never stop looking up at the night sky and hoping for a glimpse of these flying machines which come from another time and another place; far beyond the horizon of even our wildest imaginations.

CHAPTER 3

Things That Go Bump in the Night

Ghosts are a difficult subject to study. By their very nature, they are in our plane of existence for a brief moment and then they are gone before we have time to react. Ghosts are unique in the respect that the phenomenon has been reported by every culture in the history of the human race. The Bible has numerous references to ghosts, although upon closer inspection, many of these encounters actually describe demonic activity instead of the returning spirits of the dead.

Therefore, we must look at each kind of ghostly encounter and determine how the phenomena is manifesting itself before we can make educated guesses about what ghosts actually are and how they function. If we can identify the mechanism which allows or causes ghostly apparitions to appear, then we will be capable of better recording and studying the phenomena. In my experience, the majority of ghostly activity can be placed into two categories. Most paranormal investigators will disagree with me and argue that there are more categories of ghostly phenomena than the two I will mention. I am occasionally inclined to agree with them, as there are undoubtedly various subcategories to my two primary types, but just two major types will suit our purposes for now.

- Poltergeist: A seemingly intelligent entity which interacts with humans, animals and objects, sometimes in a violent manner. Poltergeists have been responsible for attacks against people, occasionally leaving physical marks on the body of their victim. They are able to move objects in the room, and will sometimes take on a physical shape, although more often they remain invisible.

- Apparition: Any other form whereby a seemingly unintelligent entity manifests itself as an odor, sound, or shape (to include shapes of animals, things, or people). Apparitions have been variously described as Crisis Apparitions, Residual Hauntings, Orbs, and plain old Ghosts. It is important to note that although apparitions may appear to be intelligent, there is much evidence which suggests that they are not. Any appearance of intelligence may just be wishful thinking on the part of the investigator.

When first investigating a haunted location, it is important to determine which type of haunting is manifesting itself. If an apparition(s) is present, then simple detection and recording equipment will be enough to begin your investigation. However, if there are violent forces at work, then your goal will be to put a stop to the activity and compel the entity to leave the location.

Due to the unpredictable nature of the poltergeist phenomena, it is more than likely that the activity will stop on its own, rather than through the intervention of an experienced paranormal investigator. However, poltergeists have been known to remain at a location for many years, and may temporarily "hibernate" for years at a time. There is much evidence to support the belief that poltergeists are actually demonic forces, and have little to do with the spirits of the recently deceased. It is also possible that a poltergeist may manifest itself in the form of an apparition some of the time, thereby confusing investigators.

Some of the tools used by paranormal investigators were originally designed for other intentions. The EMF meter, Gauss meter, and Tri-field meter are all designed to detect strong electromagnetic fields, and therefore are quite useful in detecting the presence of a ghost. An Infrared Thermometer can be used to detect changes in temperature, and is able to confirm the presence of "cold spots" which are thought to be caused by the appearance of a ghost. These tools have been in use by paranormal investigators for many years, but a good investigator should always experiment with new technologies. Two devices that I have had some success with are a stud finder and an EMF listener.

The stud finder has been referred to as the "poor mans' EMF meter" but this is technically not correct, as stud finders do not operate on the same principles as the EMF meter. A stud finder is designed to detect dense objects. If you hold a stud finder in mid-air and then slowly move it close to something, it will give off a signal. Ghosts have been reported to set off motion sensors, and therefore, we can assume that ghosts have density some of the time. A stud finder works like a portable motion detector that you can easily carry around a haunted location. While working with the TV crew from the show *Creepy Canada*, I had great success with this method, and I was especially pleased when the IR Thermometer registered changes in temperature in synch with the stud finder's readings.

An EMF listener works on the same principle as an ultrasonic leak detector, but it is infinitely more portable and user-friendly. The listener turns electro-magnetic frequencies into audible sound. When your EMF meter gets a reading, you know that something is there because you will be able to hear the sound it is making. My experimentation with this has been limited, but it is promising to consider that we may be able to hear Electronic Voice Phenomenon (EVP) while it's happening instead of having to listen to a tape later. The EMF listener is

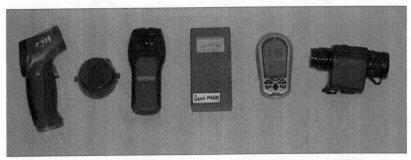

Figure 16. The tools of the trade. IR temperature gun, EMF listener, stud finder, Gauss meter, electronic compass, night vision scope.

very inexpensive, a pair, one for each ear, costs about twenty dollars.

The Ouija Board is frequently called a gateway into the spirit world, but most experts agree that the only spirits talking through the boards are "lower level" spirits who could be tricksters or demons using the beliefs of the Ouija participants to interact with humans. There are verified accounts of teenagers and adults using the Ouija board and becoming possessed by the spirits they had conjured. It is important to realize that although the spirits communicating through the board may seem genuine, you have no way to determine if they are who or what they say they are.

It is my belief that the dead cannot return to or communicate with the world of the living. The rare cases where spirits of the deceased seem to be communicating are more likely the result of a demonic force taking the form of the deceased person and attempting to fool the people who are present. This is not to say that I do not believe in ghosts or the haunting phenomena. It is a matter of semantics to emphasize that apparitions are more likely the result of residual energy replaying itself, like a video tape, for unknown reasons. What are these reasons? That is the ten million dollar question which has eluded paranormal investigators studying ghosts.

Most parapsychologists believe that people trigger or activate ghost activity, and some people, called psychics, are more sensitive to the spiritual plane. If we discount the idea of spirits returning from the dead and consider the haunting phenomenon as purely residual energy, then psychics are people who are able to "see" the recorded energy more easily than the majority of human beings. Parapsychologists usually approach hauntings by focusing their investigation on the people who are afflicted by the ghosts, rather than on the apparitions. They have concluded that the presence of increased ions and variations in the earth's magnetic field can have an adverse effect on the frontal lobe of the brain.

Frontal lobe turbulence is thought by some to actually cause the haunting to happen. However, it's far more likely that so-called psychics are simply better attuned, for whatever reason, to the energy trapped in the astral plane. I would like to mention that I totally discount the abilities of "mediums" whom I distinguish from psychics. Mediums claim the ability to communicate with the dead, and fall into two categories: either they are blatant frauds, or they are legitimate psychics who are being tricked by demonic forces acting as though they are the deceased.

What causes human energy to be trapped in a certain location is unknown, and one of the great mysteries of the ghost phenomenon. Troy Taylor really was the first person to begin to put together the idea that the presence of water will somehow affect whether a place is haunted. If we look at the most haunted places in America, we see that all of them are located near, or on top of, a major water source. Gettysburg, Pennsylvania and Alcatraz Prison are widely considered the two most haunted places in the world. The abandoned Alcatraz is situated on an island in the San Francisco Bay, completely surrounded by water. The Gettysburg Battlefield, where numerous eyewitnesses have had encounters with spectral armies, reliving the battle on the field where they died, is on top of a massive underground aquifer.

The theory is that human energy is being trapped in these water supplies like a battery holds power. Even the Bible states that water is the home of ghosts. Job 26:5 reads "The departed spirits tremble under the waters." The Hebrew word used for departed spirits in this verse is *Rephaim*, which means shades (ghosts), not demons. This energy is then released in its original form when the proper stimuli are applied. For example, if I sit in a chair and smoke a pipe every night, the energy that I expend while doing that might get caught and contained in a water source under my house. Someday someone would enter the room and see an apparition of me sitting in that chair smoking a pipe. They may even smell the pipe tobacco as a residual effect. If I happen to be dead already, then the eyewitnesses would be positive that it is my ghost returning from the dead to sit in the chair and smoke. If I am not dead, then the apparition would be considered a doppelganger, a harbinger of ill fortune which appears as a ghost of the living. There are many such accounts of living ghosts being seen all over the world.

This theory would go a long way to explain ghosts of the living, which are frequently reported. It would also explain why ghosts are almost always seen with their clothes on. Why would a returning spirit be wearing clothes? Most apparitions are seen wearing the clothes they wore in daily life, not the clothes they were wearing when they died. Do clothes have ghostly counterparts that can be purchased at the local "ghost Gap?" Of course not, that's absurd. It is far more logical that apparitions are just the result of recorded human energy being replayed.

I once encountered an apparition of my younger sister, who is still alive. My youngest sister Devin and I were walking down the upstairs hallway of our house when my sister Casey walked past both of us wearing a purple velvet dress. She didn't say anything to either of us, or acknowledge our presence; however, I felt her moving past me in the hallway. Casey walked into the bedroom at the opposite end of the hall and when Devin and I followed her, we were shocked to find that she had disappeared. Thinking she was playing a trick, we quickly searched the bedroom and then headed downstairs, only to find Casey sitting at the kitchen counter eating a sandwich and wearing totally different clothes! I do want to stress that the apparition of my sister had substance because I could actually feel her moving past me in the hallway. This cannot be explained by the conventional belief that all ghosts are spirits returning from the dead.

Some of the effects of these apparitions have convinced some paranormal investigators that ghosts have intelligence and that they are trying to communicate with the living. The most convincing and dramatic of these effects is Electronic Voice Phenomenon (EVP). I have had personal experiences with EVP and I'm convinced that it is a very real and interesting phenomenon; these experiences are discussed in detail in the Rail Road House story that appears later in this chapter.

EVP occurs when a paranormal investigator places a tape recorder, video camera, or other sound recording device in an area that is supposed to be haunted. Letting the device record for several hours, the investigator then listens to the tape and tries to find evidence of human voices which were not audible during the recording session. Such voices, it must be argued, are the result of ghosts or voices from the dead. However I believe that most EVP is simply an extension of the apparition phenomena. Human movement expends energy which is replayed as a ghostly apparition. In the same manner, human speech expends vocal energy which appears later as EVP. Some EVPs may also be from a demonic force.

Another possible causal factor in haunted locations could be the presence of high voltage wires. In at least two cases that I am personally aware of, homes that were the scene of horrendous apparition hauntings were located directly under high voltage wires. It is possible that high voltage wires capture or contain energy in the same manner as water. If this is true, then perhaps we can somehow use electricity as a means to "free" the trapped energy.

Now I would like to share four of the most fascinating cases that I have worked on during the past seven years. These cases are good examples of the different ghostly manifestations that paranormal investigators sometimes find themselves up against. It is important to remember that it has taken me seven long years to collect this evidence, and one cannot just show up at a haunted location and expect amazing results on the first try. It takes patience, hard work, and tenacity to make your research pay off.

THE WOODS OF NOXEN

In the woods surrounding Noxen, Pennsylvania, there have been reports of strange phenomena linked to the ghost of a witch that used to live in the area. The era during which she lived was the 1920s. Her name was Gertie Rhodes. She lived deep in the woods, and only left her house during the night. Gertie could be seen on any given night traveling silently through the woods with only a candle to light her way. There were even whisperings that she could talk to the animals. Children were scared to cross her path, the adults went in from their front porches when she passed by, and it was a rare event for a visitor to enter Gertie's house.

Gertie Rhodes lived to the ripe old age of 88 before being buried in a cemetery not far from the woods that she used to wander through. Locals say that she never had electricity, and was the kind of person who "left a lasting impression on you."

My team had three goals when setting up this investigation. One, find and photograph Gertie's tombstone. Two, find and photograph the remains of her house in the woods. Three, record evidence of any paranormal events that may transpire during the investigation. We succeeded in two of the three objectives.

After getting a wealth of background information from Deloris Gammon and her husband Luther, we decided to enter the woods with our cameras and notebooks. I took some Polaroids and a few black and white pictures before we left the Gammon residence and set off into the woods at four in the afternoon. George, my partner in this case, had a pretty good idea where the foundation of Gertie's house was located, so I followed after his lead. We walked about a half mile back into the woods and started to ascend a hill. Near the top of the hill, we came upon an old milk canister. George remarked that the foundation of the house was nearby and the canister probably had belonged to Gertie Rhodes.

With that, I decided to take a picture of it. I pushed the button; I heard the camera click, and then, nothing. The camera just stopped working. I couldn't get the film to advance, and I couldn't get it to take another picture. The camera was an automatic 35mm loaded with black and white film. No matter what I tried, I could not get the camera to work for the rest of our expedition. Roughly fifty yards from the milk canister, on top of the ridge, we found the foundation of Gertie's house. It

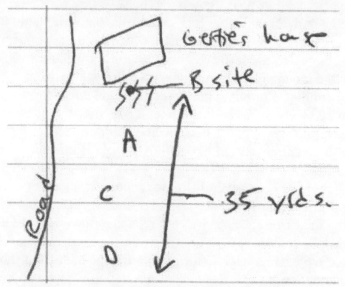

Figure 17. Field sketch of the Rhodes excavation site.

was little more than a stone floor, overgrown with grass and weeds, but there was a goldmine of refuse on the side of the structure.

As George took measurements of the foundation, I looked around the refuse that was strewn on the bank sloping away from the house. There were assorted bottles and some dishes and some tins of tobacco. I took a glass flask and wrapped it in plastic wrap. Then I took two tobacco tins and wrapped them, and then I took a broken piece of milk glass, which had been part of a serving dish. The presence of milk glass helped us date this find to 1935, the year it was no longer manufactured in large quantities. The tobacco tins were also significant because Gertie was known to have smoked and chewed tobacco. By this time, it was getting dark, so we decided to head back to the house. I was still angry that my camera wouldn't work, and I couldn't even get the film to rewind.

As we started to descend the mountain, we heard a strange sound, like a rustling in the trees. When we were standing at the foundation, this sound was to our right, along the ridge. Then, as we made our way through the dark woods, the sound moved to our left, and appeared to follow our movements down the mountainside. Whenever we stopped to listen, the sound continued moving, but we couldn't get a feel for what it might be. George has been a hunter all his life, and he said there was no way it could have been deer or any other animal, because no animal would have followed us as far as that mysterious sound. I suppose it would only be right to mention that there have been several Bigfoot encounters in this general area, so there is always the possibility that whatever was making the rustling sound was not related to the ghost of Gertie Rhodes.

We made it back to the house, and the next day I took the camera (with the film stuck in it) to a photography shop and had them remove it in a darkroom. The first five pictures came out perfectly normal but the sixth picture, the one of the milk canister, was blacked out completely. With the exception of a white streak that was placed exactly where the milk canister would have appeared in the picture. There was also a small white density to the left of the streak, which cannot be accounted for. Both anomalies are on the negative, and the guy at the photo shop has no idea what they are.

After receiving this evidence, and considering what George and I had heard while making our descent, I knew I needed to return to the woods. I came back a few weeks later with Neil, my close friend and an assistant field investigator. We decided to first visit the cemetery where Gertie was supposedly buried in an effort to find her gravestone. After nearly an hour of searching, we were empty handed. It was beginning to get pretty dark, so we left the cemetery and proceeded to the woods. Carrying only a flashlight and my camera, we plunged into the darkness. Both of us walked along

Figure 18. Neil Whitmoyer in the woods of Noxen.

quietly, prepared for anything, but not knowing what to expect. After walking in the woods for about half an hour, Neil and I decided to turn around and head back because it was simply too dark for us to see anything.

On our way out of the woods, we were hit with the most convincing and frightening evidence I have ever encountered, which has fueled my belief that there is something horrible lurking in those woods. We both heard a woman's voice laughing from deep in the woods. This was not a case of EVP. Neil and I stood there, listening, trying to make out where the voice was coming from. The laughing went on for maybe thirty seconds, and then stopped altogether. There was no way there could have been an actual person out there, as Neil and I would've heard them coming in or out of the woods.

Besides, it was past ten o'clock at night, not very agreeable conditions for a woman to be in the woods alone. I wanted to mark the occasion, so I took a picture of Neil with my flashlight held up to him. The picture, once again on black and white film, shows small globes of light behind him, which are also present on the negative. The eerie sound of a woman in those woods was enough for us. We quickly left the scene and to this day, Neil has still not returned.

George and I returned to the foundation of Gertie's house on September 4, 2000, intent on performing a full-scale excavation of the site. We conducted a second survey of the foundation area and identified four middens. For the non-archaeologists among us, a midden is a term meaning "buried refuse heap." Over the course of several hours, we successfully removed and catalogued thirty-five individual artifacts, all dating from the same time period as the earlier artifacts we found.

The more significant items were taken from the dig site and cleaned up for further study. Midden D yielded the most artifacts, the majority of which were buried underneath a tree. Among these items was what appeared to be a perfume bottle, listed as artifact D4. When I uncovered this artifact, I held it up to get a better look at it and as I did, the wind picked up and I felt what I thought were leaves falling out of the tree onto my back. George walked over to my side to look at the bottle and instead shouted "Worms!" We were both covered with little green worms which had fallen out of the tree when the wind started blowing. After brushing each other off, we decided to leave the perfume bottle behind and carted the collection of artifacts back to civilization.

I was unable to return to the foundation site again until November 2001. My goal this time was to recover artifacts D4 and D7, which had been previously left behind. On the path leading to the foundation, there were several places where the leaves had been cleared away and a strange symbol was scratched into the dirt. There were at least three occurrences of this symbol starting directly in front of the foundation and ending just after the milk jug. I have done some research and tried to identify the symbol, but I have had no success in finding its meaning.

While leaving the site, again, I heard the strange sound from the ridge which appeared to be following me through the woods. I wanted to confront whatever it was, so I left the trail and began to climb up the steep ridge. After I had climbed about halfway up the mountain, the sound stopped, so I turned around and headed back to the path. Although, upon returning to the trail, I realized that I had lost or dropped the D4 artifact somewhere along the way. It would appear that this mysterious perfume bottle is somehow connected to the ghostly phenomenon that is occurring in those woods.

My final trip into the Noxen woods was made with an array of equipment which I was hoping to use to document some of the strange things that had happened to us. Hiking back into the deep woods over a high mountain with a tripod, two video cameras, and a host of other devices in the cold of winter was no easy task, but I managed to get back to the foundation site without too much trouble. Unfortunately, the dig site which we had so carefully excavated in 2000 was now totally destroyed by a logging crew who had recently started a timber clearing operation throughout the wooded area.

Their machines were working the day of my visit, so attempting to gather EVP would've been impossible, and I was not about to leave my equipment running so the loggers could steal it while I was off investigating the ridge. Considering the complete destruction of five years of our hard work and the likelihood that the logging operations would continue for the foreseeable future, I was forced to permanently close the case of Gertie Rhodes. May she rest in peace, wherever she may be.

MARIETTA RAIL ROAD HOUSE

Located in Marietta, Pennsylvania, the Railroad House Restaurant, Bed and Breakfast was built in the early 1820s to provide lodging and refreshment for the travelers on the Portage Railroad, which still runs directly in front of the building. The hotel flourished until the Great Depression when it was forced to go out of business, but it was reopened in the late 1970s after extensive restorations, and today it serves as a fine dining restaurant and a bed and breakfast.

For several years, Rick Fisher, head of the Paranormal Society of Pennsylvania, has with the cooperation of the owners conducted an intense investigation of the entire Railroad House property. His findings (EVP, photographic evidence, and chronicling of eyewitness accounts) continue to inspire and amaze new generations of ghost hunters.

On January 3rd, 2004, I was invited to spend a night on the haunted property with Rick's team, learning from their methods and helping with the investigation. I was given the unpleasant task of spending eight hours alone in the cottage house, a small building separate from the main hotel that was once a summer kitchen, but is now used as a quaint honeymoon cottage.

Guests to the cottage have reported the ghost of an old woman sitting in a rocking chair, and Rick later learned that a

Figure 19. Bottom floor of the Cottage House.

young boy drowned in a well that used to be in front of the cottage. The cottage consists of a large open room with a spiral staircase leading to an open loft on the second floor where a rocking chair has been placed to accommodate the old woman's apparition.

We set up a video camera and a tape recorder in the loft, and a night vision camera and an EMF meter on the bottom floor; in addition, I hand-carried a 35mm film camera for photographs, and an IR temperature gun. While in the cottage house, I reported hearing a "click" upstairs at 9:20 p.m. and made a note that the room felt "cold," although there were no adverse readings on the temperature gun, nor was there any activity on the EMF meter. The entire time I was in the cottage house, I felt uneasy, although I wrote it off as psychological jitters. When my eight hours in the cottage were finished, I kept the tapes rolling and left for a few minutes, to see if anything might happen and be recorded while I was gone.

The resulting video tape and audio tapes yielded amazing evidence of a ghostly presence. Numerous EVPs were found on both sets of tape, and on the video, a ball of light can clearly be seen running across the floor *through* the legs of the

Figure 20. Loft of the Cottage House.

rocking chair! I was able to capture five different occurrences of EVP during my eight hours in the cottage. The first was the voice of a woman saying something in garbled speech, nothing conclusive.

Before sending me out on my own, Rick had instructed me to occasionally talk with the ghosts. Even though I couldn't hear their responses, it's one way to get activity to show up on the tape. So, I did. At one point, while I was sitting on top of the staircase, I said "I'm gonna sit down stairs for a little while." In response, on the audio tape, a male voice responded by saying "Why don'tcha come here first?" and then that is followed by a low groaning sound. When I heard this particular track later, it just made my skin crawl. It was very creepy.

Later, also while I was sitting at the top of the steps, I was trying to rouse whatever might be there, so I started casually insulting any potential entities in the room. Just before I said "I take it you don't follow orders very well," a male voice said "Get out." Not in deep demonic tones like you would expect from a Hollywood thriller, but in a calm, firm, whispered voice.

74

As if these voices weren't frightening enough, probably the most chilling voice that was heard on the tapes was that of a young boy inside the cottage. I was standing downstairs by the door, getting ready to leave. Continuing in my course of speaking to the ghosts, I said "I'm leaving the last drop of my coffee for you, if you get thirsty, don't hesitate to drink it." And in response the voice of a young boy said "What's he doin'?" No matter what skeptics might say or think, there was no little boy anywhere near that cottage that night, neither inside nor out. It is truly something from the realm of the paranormal. This same voice continued to speak after I left the cottage, although we could not be sure of what he was saying.

Amazed by my early success in capturing EVP, Rick decided to enter the cottage again with me and although nothing was heard while we investigated the tiny building, at one point the voice of a woman saying "Come here" can clearly be heard on the audio tape right after Rick finishes speaking.

So it would seem that the Marietta Rail Road House is home to numerous apparitions. As further evidence for this, Rick Fisher has collected many additional EVPs which point to several distinct presences on the property. While some might think that the "response" EVPs I recorded indicate an intelligent entity, keep in mind that we have no idea if the recorder simply picked up audio from the past that was replaying itself, or if there was a poltergeist present in the room which was making itself known.

I have not returned to the Rail Road House since participating in the investigation with Rick's group, although he has since informed me that the location is now under new ownership and he will have to work out new arrangements to see if he will still be able to continue his investigation of the property. Although one can guess that after spending a few nights in the Rail Road House alone, the new owners will be begging Rick to come back with all his cameras rolling.

THE HAUNTED SORORITY HOUSE

In an unassuming house in Bloomsburg, Pennsylvania on a random summer night in the year 2000, a young girl was the alleged victim of a terrible spiritual attack. Our investigators were the first to arrive on the scene and document evidence of the attack. Their story goes something like this:

One night, around 1:00 a.m., three girls returned home from a concert. Roommates Jodi and Amanda both climbed into their separate beds in the same room on the second floor. Jodi was sleeping soundly on the top bunk of her bunk bed. Amanda was across the room, also sound asleep.

At 3:30 a.m., Jodi found herself on the floor, and the top bunk bed lying on top of her. Amanda recalls being woken up by a scream and a loud crash. There was no damage to the bed, and our investigators determined that it was picked up and then turned over in mid-air. The posts that were supposed to hold the top bunk in place were not damaged in any way. We documented large bruises on Jodi's leg and arms. She also had scratches on her back, but she couldn't explain how they got there.

Figure 21. The haunted sorority house.

76

During our interviews with the girls who were in the house that night, we found out that other girls living in the sorority house have seen and heard strange things. One girl saw the ghost of a man wearing 1920s clothes in a downstairs room, and another remembered her door mysteriously opening on its own one night. While these stories are not conclusive proof that a ghost is haunting the residence, there is always the possibility that a poltergeist is at work.

If nothing else, the violent attack was real. The bruise on Jodi's leg was enormous, and the bunk bed could not have fallen apart on its own. There was no one in the house that night with the strength to lift the bed up in mid-air (to avoid damaging the dowel rods attaching the top bunk to the bottom bunk) and flip it onto the ground. Besides, Amanda, the only other person in the room, would've noticed someone fleeing the scene.

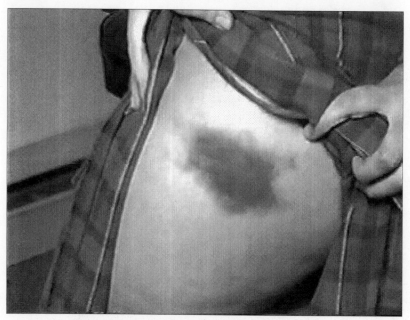

Figure 22. Large bruise on Jodi's upper thigh.

This event is a clear-cut poltergeist attack against the girl, but we were unable to determine why the attack occurred when it did, and why Jodi was the victim. I made myself available for further investigation of the house should any further bizarre events occur, but the girls from the sorority have never called me. I can only assume that the presence either left completely, or is simply laying dormant, waiting for the right moment to make another attack.

WEATHERLY CEMETERY

Weatherly Cemetery is located near the town of Hazleton, along the back roads in rural northern central Pennsylvania. If you don't know where you're going, it can be very difficult to find, and most first-time visitors drive right past it, missing the location completely. This cemetery is very run down, and the scene of numerous vandalized grave markers. St. Joseph's Catholic Church, built in 1852, once stood beside the cemetery, but it fell into disuse and was afterwards found burned to the ground in 1966. I was first told of the existence of Weatherly Cemetery by a friend who explained that it was a "witch's cemetery" and that several accused witches had been hung from a tree that stood on the grounds of the cemetery.

Neil and I were intrigued by the stories, and became determined to find the place. We set out late one night and after driving around in the dark for several hours looking for Church Road, we finally stumbled upon the cemetery. The most striking thing about Weatherly Cemetery is the total state of disarray it is in. The majority of tombstones are tipped over or otherwise vandalized, but even the stones that are still standing seem to have been placed there without any consistent pattern. Most grave plots are set in orderly lines; however, this cemetery has no order to it at all.

Figure 23. Weatherly Cemetery during the day.

I have made numerous visits to Weatherly Cemetery over the past seven years, and something out of the ordinary has happened on nearly every occasion. After posting some information about my investigation of the cemetery, I began receiving a multitude of reports from seemingly normal people who have had bizarre experiences there. A few of the visitors to the cemetery who said they saw nothing strange admitted that they felt scared the entire time they were at the location, but could not rationalize their fear.

The first person to contact me was Anne, a young girl who lived in the local area. She claimed to have seen "a man [wearing 1800s clothes] tossing logs into a pile. I lost sight of him after I got out of the car. We stood there, talking about where the church might have been and this horrible smell came over us ... That is the LAST time I went there." Three other witnesses have reported seeing the apparition of an old man dressed in old fashioned clothing standing near the road. One of them said that the apparition chased them into their car and, fantastically, grabbed one member of their party, causing him to fall to the ground. Another person claims that after watching several orbs give a spectacular light show, his car wouldn't start and he was forced to push start it in order to leave.

At my insistence, Anne returned to Weatherly on several occasions with her camera. Two of the photographs she took show anomalous shapes. On one picture, there are what appear to be two humanoid forms walking through the cemetery. She is so far the only person to offer me solid photograph proof of a ghostly presence at Weatherly.

During my onsite investigations, I have heard strange sounds coming from the woods that surround the cemetery. These sounds are like an animal moving through the leaves, however, whenever I approach the wooded area, the sounds stop, and there is no evidence suggesting that an animal was recently nearby. On one occasion, Neil and I found weird tracks in the snow which we were able to follow across the width of the cemetery, moving from the wooded area and crossing the road where they abruptly stopped. This is consistent with reports of a bizarre animal which has been seen around Weatherly Cemetery. I even have one account of a strange skull being found, which seemed to belong to a small animal, but with horns and a distorted face.

There have also been accounts of pagan rituals being performed at the cemetery.

One eyewitness recalled his story of seeing such a ritual one night. "…across the street from the cemetery in the woods, there was a bon fire, with people gathered around, we did not go back to check it out…" This is the same individual who claimed, at an earlier date, to have seen a figure wearing a black robe running down the road towards him and his friends.

A sixty-year-old friend of Anne's who no longer lives in the Hazleton area recently told her about an herb garden that was growing in the woods on the right side of the cemetery. He had no idea how this garden, which was supposedly filled with herbs used in Wicca rituals, had come to be planted, nor who maintained the garden. Anne and I have been unable to locate this garden, although I went searching during the winter, which would have made it more difficult to find.

The satanic cult that is rumored to lurk around the cemetery is said to protect it from outsiders. My friend Phil has reported being followed to and from the location by a white pickup truck. On one occasion, while I was there with a group of interested friends, a white Ford Escort drove past the cemetery and stopped to watch us. Upon seeing this, and remembering the rumors, I decided it would be best for all of us to leave immediately. As we approached our own car, the Ford Escort took off down the road. We began to drive away when we noticed that the car had turned around and was now heading back towards us. This car followed us at a close distance, even when we started speeding in an attempt to get away. Taking truly evasive action, we successfully lost our pursuers and left the area with no further trouble.

Figure 24. The "hanging tree" located at the far end of the cemetery.

Figure 25. Neil Whitmoyer looks at a stone flower pot in Weatherly Cemetery on a snowy night.

I have never posted this story anywhere, with the hope that others would come forward on their own with similar stories of being chased by white vehicles. One such person did contact me, but the vehicle he saw is quite unusual. "I was driving down the street where the cemetery is and my son started to beep the horn. All of a sudden, a white hearse showed up behind me and started driving faster … my heart was pounding … I got to the end of the road and it was gone." My subsequent communications with the witness suggest that he is telling the truth, and his son verifies his story.

In 2002, I was contacted by a local journalist who explained that his research of the cemetery proves that there were never any witches hung there. The large "hanging tree" which dominates Weatherly Cemetery is nothing more than an object of local folklore. He insists that if there are any spirits appearing at the cemetery, they are the result of local Indian burial grounds. The Lenni Lenape tribe had many camps in the area surrounding Weatherly and it is quite possible that they were using the location as a burial site long before white settlers ever arrived.

During my last visit to Weatherly Cemetery, I decided to attempt to capture EVP. Although the battery on my video camera went dead after thirty minutes and no strange sounds were recorded, I did catch three extreme temperature changes. The ambient temperature was nine degrees below zero (Fahrenheit), and the changes ranged from a twenty-four degree drop to a dramatic jump of one hundred and three degrees. An unexplained rise in temperature is usually associated with the presence of an evil entity, such as a poltergeist or something demonic. Perhaps the cultists unleashed some terrible demonic force that now stalks through the cemetery.

As a parting shot, I would like to mention a newspaper story which brought me minor grief after it was published. The headline of the July 18, 2004 edition of the *Scranton Times-Leader* read *Sacred Ground, A Look Back: St. Joseph's Catholic Church Cemetery*. The reporter who wrote the story described me and all other paranormal investigators as grave robbing vandals who do more harm than good to cemeteries. Adding insult to injury, the reporter used the text from my website to bolster her story, and then threw in interviews from the caretaker who ranted against paranormal investigators. All this was stacked against me, and yet she did not even bother to attempt to get my side of the story. Naturally, I contacted her editor to demand an explanation, but he contends that her rights are protected by the Fair Use Act, and that the text on my website did not explicitly say "this information is copyrighted."

Based on the numerous eyewitness accounts, the photographic evidence and my own experiences, I can definitely say that there is a paranormal phenomenon present at Weatherly Cemetery. The exact nature of this ghostly presence is unknown, but with more research and investigation, I believe we can determine what is responsible for the hauntings. To the waylaid traveler who finds themselves on the lonely road leading to the Weatherly Cemetery, I have the following advice. If it's dark outside, your best bet is to just keep driving. The cemetery will still be there for you to visit in the morning, trust me.

Figure 26. Old photograph of Weatherly Cemetery showing where St. Joseph's Catholic Church used to stand.

CHAPTER 4

The Witch Doctor of Wapwallopen

doctor \'dak-tər\ *n* 2a: one skilled or specializing in healing arts
witch \wich\ *n* (bef. 12c) 4: a practitioner of Wicca
witch doctor *n* (1718): a professional worker of magic

This chapter is divided into two parts. The first part details the journey I took investigating Dr. Santee's past and the interesting people I've met along the way. The second part is a concise biography of Dr. Santee's life. It should be noted that the information contained in this report would not be accurate were it not for the help of a great many persons with inside knowledge of Dr. Santee's background. The names of these people have all been changed, as have the names of everyone referenced here who is still alive. This is simply to protect their desired anonymity.

My friend Phil Karns first presented me with the case of Dr. Frederick Santee. Phil is a practicing Wiccan and is very knowledgeable about all matters of the occult and religion in general. The introduction of Dr. Santee's past came as we traveled to visit the cemetery where he's buried in Wapwallopen, Pennsylvania. Essentially, Phil told me three key points: First, that before he died, Dr. Santee had been the leader of an evil coven that practiced several kinds of black magic. Second, that his coven is still active and watches over the cemetery where he is buried, occasionally practicing their rituals on the cemetery grounds at night. Thirdly, that his house in Wapwallopen is abandoned and has two stone lion statues in front of the porch, and inside the house are Dr. Santee's collection of old books about witchcraft.

The investigation into these events lasted almost seven years but has finally come to a close. My original intentions in pursuing this case were to find the books Dr. Santee had and to study them for historic occult value. Also, to identify or catch in the act, practicing members of his coven and stop their evil rituals from occurring. Finally, to discover the source of the evil magic Dr. Santee was said to wield. In one manner or another, all three of my goals have been accomplished as will be attested to in this chapter.

THE BEGINNING

In 1997, I visited the Old River Church Cemetery with Phil Karns, Neil Whitmoyer and another friend. We were going to see, for the first time, Dr. Santee's grave. Phil had been to the cemetery once before and thus he led the way. It was rather late, and I'm honestly not sure what we expected to find there. Boredom, more than anything, had prompted our journey that night.

The cemetery sits on a small hill across the river from the PP&L power plant. There are high-tension wires hovering high above it and they are constantly humming with energy. Lights from the power plant illuminate the area surrounding the cemetery and its external announcing system can be heard clearly from the road. The only parking for the cemetery is a gravel lot that's about a two-minute walk from the actual cemetery grounds.

After arriving, we continued listening to Phil's limited background knowledge of Dr. Santee's life. All the creepy details were truly setting the stage for a late-night walk in the cemetery. The Old River Church sits directly to the left of the

Figure 29. Old River Church Cemetery, the final resting place of Dr. Santee and his wife.

cemetery and is indeed quite old. It is my understanding that the church is no longer regularly attended but is occasionally used for historical reenactments by a community church group. We bypassed the building on this trip and headed straight for the cemetery.

As we approached the wrought iron fence surrounding the cemetery, Phil carefully issued instructions for entering the gate: Whoever opened the gate had to close it after everyone else entered. If you didn't follow this guidance, the evil spirits lurking around the cemetery would make terrible things happen. Phil's belief was based in superstition more than anything else.

Dr. Santee's grave was not difficult to find. We walked up the sloping hill to the top of the cemetery where only a few graves dotted the landscape. There, under a large pine tree, was the unremarkable grave of Dr. Santee and his wife, Betty. Among the dead flowers resting in front of the headstone, there was a small decorative pot and a small plastic statue of the character Maleficent from the movie *Sleeping Beauty*. This was really just a toy from a happy meal, but I believe it was intended to represent a witch and was most likely placed there by local teenagers who were familiar with Dr. Santee's legend.

"I shall return when spring's first shadow trails" was the epitaph on the headstone. Phil began telling us that the epitaph was originally something else, but then one day, it mysteriously turned into the present saying. At first hearing, I was dubious of this claim. A simple explanation would be that Santee's friends/family wanted to change the epitaph and did so at their convenience. The minor mystery Phil presented concerning the headstone has never really troubled me and it was never pursued.

However, the meaning behind the epitaph is far more intriguing. It seems to say that the doctor or his wife will return from the dead "when spring's first shadow trails." My first impression was that the epitaph was meant as an instruction for his coven to resurrect his soul or maybe even his person on a certain date corresponding with the passing of the spring equinox. This was my main theory for many years until I discovered that the epitaph is simply a line from one of Dr.

Figure 30. Dr. Santee's grave.

Santee's unpublished poems.

That night, I left the cemetery genuinely intrigued about Dr. Santee and his past. Phil later took us to Dr. Santee's former house, which I later discovered was not really his house at all, but was on the same street as his actual house. He also drove us by the "Head Witch's" house. This "Head Witch" was supposedly the current leader of the Wapwallopen coven and was extremely dangerous. So, from the very beginning, I was instilled with the belief that Dr. Santee was an evil coven leader who was surrounded by demonic spirits and sadistic coven members.

FIRST RESEARCH AND FIELD WORK

The first task on my list was to visit Dr. Santee's grave during the day to make a rubbing of the headstone and get a better look around. After this, I visited the local library and scrolled through a few reams of microfilm looking for the obituaries of Dr. Santee and his wife. The obituaries were interesting in several respects. It was here, in the pages of the *Bloom Times*, that I got my first look at my quarry. Santee's obituary had his picture and gave me a solid background for further research into his past. Betty's obituary was smaller, but yielded a few clues about her surviving relatives, namely, a stepdaughter identified as Mrs. Juan Zaragoza.

My initial attempts at finding Juan Zaragoza were unfruitful and came to nothing more than a dead end. I returned to the Santee gravesite and, in the character of Indiana Jones, took the witch statue. This proved to be one of the most irresponsible things I've done in my pursuit for the truth, and I later regretted my actions. After turning the statue over to Phil, he berated me for my actions and gave it to his friend Wes, who I believe was also a practicing Wiccan. Apparently on the first night Wes had the statue in his house, he was tormented by terrible nightmares. These haunting visions prompted Wes to return the statue the following day. I cannot say for certain what caused Wes's nightmares, but I suspect it was a subconscious psychological reaction to the presence of what Wes believed was an "evil object." It should be noted that about a month after the statue was returned, it disappeared along with the small ceramic pot. These objects were most likely removed by either the caretaker or local teenagers.

I returned to the Santee gravesite on Halloween night, the witch's sabbat of Samhain. This night holds great attraction for pagan religions, as it is the night when the spirit world comes closest to ours. If ever there was a night to catch a coven in action, this was it. Neil and I headed to the cemetery and arrived just before midnight. The parking lot was full of cars, which was not a good sign. We drove by the cemetery grounds, but because of the sloping hill, our view was obstructed. Neil and I both believed Santee's coven was there, practicing a ritual around his grave, perhaps trying to resurrect his spirit. It clearly was in our best interest to leave the area, as there had to be at least ten people there, and none with good intentions.

Several months later, we returned to the cemetery. Our goal this time was to show up earlier in the night and wait in the woods, watching over the gravesite until the coven members returned. This way, we could observe their activities from a safe vantage point and minimize the risk of a potentially dangerous confrontation. The surveillance mission yielded nothing, as no one showed up for us to watch.

Eventually, my interest in Dr. Santee died down. I visited the cemetery and the small town of Wapwallopen sparingly during the following years, usually out of boredom more than anything else. Occasionally, I would talk to Phil and he might mention something about Dr. Santee, but other than that, it was a cold case.

In September of 2002, I paid a nighttime visit to the Old River Church Cemetery with Neil and our mutual friend Julie. We hadn't been to the cemetery in almost a year, and I wanted to show Julie Dr. Santee's grave. It was a cold night when we walked down the road towards the cemetery grounds. As we approached the edge of the church driveway, we all heard movement coming from the woods less than fifty yards away. The three of us stopped in our tracks and listened quietly.

A gunshot rang out from the woods, shattering the quiet, sending us running back to our car. We got in and drove back past the cemetery. I was pretty angry, and I wanted to find out if someone had really been firing at us. The blast sounded like a shotgun and it was possible they fired at us and missed or just fired in the air to scare us off. We saw nothing as we drove past the section of woods where the shot had originated. We all agreed that none of us wanted to return to the cemetery and our expedition was put to an abrupt halt.

This unusual confrontation prompted me to resume my investigation. Obviously someone was watching over the gravesite. It may just have been local teenagers, but more likely, it was the coven members. Later that week, I visited Wapwallopen, hoping to find Dr. Santee's house. I knew it was at 5 River Street, and I also knew that the house Phil had shown me was not the right place. I parked my car at the end of River Street and began walking towards the post office about four blocks away.

The house closest to the post office turned out to be 5 River Street, indicated by a small sign in the front yard. The book house, a small library where Santee was said to practice his rituals, was a concrete building adjacent to the main house. No one appeared to be home, although after the events in the cemetery, I was unwilling to press for any further confrontations with potentially dangerous people.

As I stopped to take a few pictures of Dr. Santee's house and book house, a woman who appeared to be in her thirties emerged from the apartment across the street and started smoking a cigarette while two cats played at her feet (this becomes significant later). She watched me as I finished taking pictures and continued to walk down the street. I made eye contact with her only once and it was very obvious she was suspicious of my actions. By the time I reached my car and

Figure 31. Dr. Santee's former residence at 5 River Street.

drove back down the street, she and her feline companions had retreated inside. My immediate thought was that this woman was a member of the Santee coven.

I continued my research of Dr. Santee on the Internet. The old newspaper reports were going nowhere, and I wanted to find new information. A cursory search brought me to a genealogy post left by Chaz Brubaker, a Pennsylvania man who was looking for information about Dr. Santee. Naturally, I contacted Mr. Brubaker and we engaged in a mutual exchange of information. He had a lot of things I didn't, such as Santee's will and a copy of his book *The Devil's Wager*. Brubaker had apparently been investigating the Santee coven for the past fifteen years.

After several weeks of e-mails, I felt I had enough new information to publish a web page about Dr. Santee. My communication with Brubaker eventually died down and I assumed he would contact me if any new information came up. The web page had been public for about three months when I got an e-mail from a woman named Laura who claimed to have been a former patient of Santee's when she was a child.

Laura recounted her experiences at the Santee clinic, which had been in his house. Her insight was very valuable and she raised a few questions about his general behavior in the clinic. She said: "I remember that he used to make me sit on his lap and he asked my mother if I could work for him when I turned twelve. I have a memory of seeing his library and being upstairs with a bunch of kids who were apparently living there. I can also remember him giving my aunt a shot in the neck (right under the chin). I'm a nurse now and I still have no idea what that was for."

The kids living upstairs were most likely college students, as Brubaker informed me that he was once contacted by an anthropology grad student who had lived with Santee in the 1970s and was "taught a few things by doctor Fred, but promised to keep what he learned a secret, more out of respect for Santee than out of some fearful oath."

Laura continued relaying her childhood memories of visits to Santee's home clinic, saying that the front yard was filled with baby copper heads, his receptionist was young and pretty and one of his nurses had a rubber nose and long gray hair. She further speculated on rumors heard around town: "As I got older I heard rumors that he performed abortions, sold drugs and had séances in his house ... I always wondered if the rumors are true. I also heard that he studied the words or works of some famous old Indian who supposedly cursed the whole Wyoming Valley."

At one point, Dr. Santee was investigated by the DEA, but nothing ever came of it. This is probably where the rumors of him selling drugs originated. Although he did dispense his own medicine to patients, this doesn't seem irregular for a doctor with a private clinic. Séances would be a normal activity for the leader of a coven, perhaps slightly unusual for a doctor, but altogether not too bizarre. It simply lends more credibility to the likelihood that Dr. Santee was involved in occult practices.

On March 16th, 2003, I received my first e-mail from an individual who would help blow the lid off every theory I'd ever synthesized about Dr. Santee's past. G. Hoke, a self-described *3rd High Priest in Celtic/Germanic Wicca*, had found the webpage I'd created about Santee and decided to contact me to set the story straight. His opening paragraph made it very clear where he stood on the subject: "The Wicca we practice and that was practiced at the Doctor's Covenstead has nothing to do with Satanism or evil, I assure you."

This was the biggest break I'd gotten in six years. One of my objectives was to contact a member of the coven to learn more about their activities first hand. Hoke agreed to provide me with all the information I wanted if I would remove the webpage, which he considered slanderous. I gladly did as he requested and we engaged in sessions of *quid pro quo* over the following days.

Upon informing Brubaker about these new developments in the investigation, he told me that he had directed a member of Santee's coven to my webpage, and that that person had passed the information onto G. Hoke. Brubaker went on to confess that his intention from day one had been to establish contact with a member of the coven in hopes of joining the sect and reviving the lineage in his local area. At the very least, I felt betrayed. Brubaker had played me like a fiddle and I didn't even see it, he had used me (and my investigative team) to dispel the mysteries and secrecy surrounding Dr. Santee in order to serve his own personal agenda. The fact that his agenda ran counter to mine only made it worse.

At this point, I decided to abandon my communications with Brubaker and focus on getting what I could from Hoke, who now wanted to send me an eight page biography of Dr. Santee that had been written using numerous sources, including two of Santee's Harvard Yearbooks, a master's thesis about the coven Hoke had found in the book house, and first-hand accounts of the doctor from people who knew him, mostly coven members. I should mention that G. Hoke never actually knew Dr. Santee, but joined the coven shortly after Santee died and thus had unfettered access to most of his materials.

We continued corresponding for several days and I gained a wealth of new information about Santee from G. Hoke. He answered to my satisfaction all the questions posed about events surrounding the cemetery and the present state of the coven. In response to my concerns about the large number of cars outside the cemetery on the evening of the Sabbat, Hoke says, "I assure you the two ladies in their 80s who are the surviving members of the old Coven up there weren't stalking around his grave in the cold and dark at midnight ... Most likely this was teenagers who traditionally go to graveyards on this holiday to scare themselves and their girlfriends!"

However, he contradicted this statement in an earlier correspondence. "The Coven of the Catta (cat totem) still exists as two older Witches in the Nescopeck and Berwick areas, and in the dozen or so initiated into that lineage who live in the Harrisburg area ... We witches just want to worship the Goddess and celebrate the changing seasons in peace." It is, in my opinion, more than probable that a dozen or so members of the Santee coven gathered at his gravesite to celebrate the changing season on the Fall Equinox.

He elaborates further, indicating that there are several women connected with Santee who still live in the area. "I have been to the grave where he is buried and the flowers are probably from one of several ladies who still live nearby and were librarians, nurses and Witches in his Coven." The idea of the nurses being involved in the coven is expounded upon in the text of the master's thesis. "He [Santee] seems to have been pushed into HighPriest position to please his girls ... although HPS should be leader actually Santee was the leader." G. Hoke did, however, confirm that the "Head Witch" does not currently live in Wapwallopen.

When Hoke read about Wes's nightmares while he had been in possession of the stolen witch statue, he said "There may be some paranormal activity around the gravesite especially when someone comes and steals objects from his grave ... I assure you there are still some protective energies there." G. Hoke further confirmed that the current owners of Santee's house have no interest in Wicca, but are distant relatives of a former coven founder.

I was curious to know his thoughts on Brubaker and the man's intention of joining the coven. Hoke said, "There is no need for him to come to the rescue of the Coven, which is alive and well, though small, and not actively recruiting new members." So, I presume Brubaker's goal was squashed before he got too far.

While still in contact with Hoke, I received an e-mail from a woman identifying herself as "Lady Phoebe," who is one of two original coven members still alive, and furthermore, was a part-founder of the Santee coven. My correspondence with this woman was productive and helped bring closure to the investigation into Dr. Santee's past. Lady Phoebe began by dispelling the rumors about Santee and by saying that she had worked for him for over half her life. She said my sources were sadly misinformed and, "There wasn't an evil bone in his [Santee's] body."

Lady Phoebe was apparently Dr. Santee's soul mate and closest friend. Her words show just how much she admired him. "He was the kindest individual anyone would want to meet and he would never harm a living soul. Frederick was the most gentle and humble man, outside of my father. Wapwallopen area folks were blessed to have this man tend to their sick." I believed her sincerity and the fact that she was the only person I'd corresponded with who called him Frederick showed me how close they must've been.

Much of what Lady Phoebe told me reinforced Hoke's statements and the eight-page document he had sent me. I got the impression she had never read the document because some of the things she told me didn't match up. This, she explained, was because G. Hoke never had any personal contact with Santee, while she knew him "inside and out." Our correspondence continued, but most of my questions about

Santee had already been answered by Hoke, so I instead focused on Santee's living descendants.

I have agreed to keep what Lady Phoebe told me about Santee's daughter/granddaughters confidential, and I will make every effort to keep that promise while discussing this subject. My original intention in seeking this information was to try and find Santee's granddaughters to interview them. However, I no longer feel this is necessary as Lady Phoebe, G. Hoke, Brubaker and everyone else I've interviewed have provided more than enough information to fill in the missing pieces. Concerning the granddaughters, Lady Phoebe said that she was in regular contact with Santee's daughter until the woman died. Furthermore, Santee's granddaughters are currently living in another part of the country but they still keep in touch with Lady Phoebe, although not as much as they used to.

After I published the first edition of this story, Lady Phoebe requested that I send her a copy for her review. I did, hoping that she could correct any glaring errors I had made about the Doctor's life. She later responded by asking me to call her so we could discuss the details of Santee's past. It took me a few days to finally work up the courage to dial her phone number, but I am truly glad I did.

A weak but steady voice greeted me that evening of April first, and after I introduced myself, the elderly female responded by saying "I am the Lady Phoebe."

It was truly a momentous occasion. Having the opportunity to speak with the Head Witch of Santee's coven meant that all my questions would be answered, and I could be sure of hearing the truth. She began by telling me that just before he died, Santee had said to her, "Please dear, write about me and you and tell the truth." It was a request that she took seriously, and had it not been for the interference of others, Lady Phoebe's version of Santee's biography would've already been published. I will always be grateful to her for the insight into the Doctor's life she provided to me. It was the chance to see Frederick through the eyes of someone who had shared her life with him, and with whom she shared a "pure love."

Directly following my conversation with Lady Phoebe, Bobbie, one of Santee's former patients, who remembered a lot about her childhood physician, contacted me. "He was an excellent doctor, and whatever he had prescribed sure had worked, and fast." She went on to comment on his home office, lending support to Laura's earlier description. "His office I remember was 'spooky' and the girls I found to be 'strange,' rumors were that they were 'his witches.'" Her statements, I later discovered, are only partially correct. While several of the nurses were formal members of the coven, a few others were only observers, occasionally watching the Wicca rituals that Santee conducted in his basement and book house.

Bobbie went on to recount a story about her brother, saying that he was once romantically involved with one of Santee's nurses. "My brother got involved with … the one nurse and he told a lot of strange stories." Thinking that he might have some relevant information to share with me, Bobbie contacted him. Their conversation was intriguing, to say the least. "I tried to speak to him yesterday," she said, "and he became very frightened and refused to talk with me, he said he does not even want to think about that part of his life."

The information Bobbie provided me eventually led me to another former nurse, Maria. An unsolicited letter was my only shot at getting any information from Maria, so I sent a list of questions to her, trying to corroborate some of the details I'd recently picked up so I could finally pull the entire story together. She wrote me back several weeks later, and provided a few snippets to help me finish my work.

The fruit of my labors is contained in the following pages. I am fairly certain that the biography of Dr. Santee I have compiled is the most complete and accurate to date. While there are others out there who know far more than I do about this particular subject, they have chosen to remain in the shadows. It has been my pleasure to dig into this mystery, even if what I found was less than sensational.

Frederick Santee was no more evil than your average person, and he didn't conduct satanic rituals. He did, undoubtedly, possess a range of unusual characteristics, and these were well known because of his prominent position in the small community in which he made his home. Dr. Santee was a witch, or warlock to be more precise, but that didn't make him a bad doctor or a bad person, just a different kind of person; one who comes along every so often that everybody remembers, but no one ever talks about. As one of his former patients remarked, "What a strange and interesting man he was."

A BIOGRAPHY OF DR. FREDERICK LAMOTTE SANTEE

In his own words this is "a story of repeated attempts to root myself somewhere, of repeated failures to hold fast to my chosen career as a college teacher, in a world in which few can be taught, fewer still want to be, and a socialistic habit of thought reduces even those few to uniform patters of empty gesture."

Frederick Santee's grandfather, Ephraim A. Santee, was born in Luzerne County, Pennsylvania on 8 July, 1837 to John and Rebecca Santee. The son of a second-generation farmer, he began to study medicine in 1861 with Dr. A. L. Cressler at Jefferson Medical College where he remained until his graduation in 1869. During the American Civil War, he became a medical cadet in the army and his primary duty was as assistant surgeon. Shortly after he began attending Jefferson, Ephraim married Thankful R. Post of Union Township, Pennsylvania.

Ephraim first practiced medicine in Lehman, Pennsylvania until 1866 and then moved to Shickshinny. In October 1870, he left Shickshinny for Hollenback and in May of 1872, moved on to Hobbie where he entered into a partnership with Dr. Price in 1878. Records show Ephraim registered his practice with the Luzurne County Homeopathic Society in 1881 when a law was passed requiring all practicing physicians to do so. Finally, in 1886, he moved one last time, to Wapwallopen and died of senile debility on 16 September 1915. He left behind his wife Thankful and three children, James, Susie and Charles.

Ephraim's son, Charles LaMotte Santee, was born 1876, and followed in his father's footsteps by practicing medicine. Charles studied medicine first at LaFayette and also at the same college as his father, Jefferson Medical, earning his M.D. there in 1901. After earning his medical degree, Charles subsequently enrolled in the postgraduate obstetrics program at Johns Hopkins University in Baltimore. The education he received there later served him very well, as he gained a reputation for never losing a child or mother during the birthing process.

During World War I, Charles followed the family military tradition that would later be carried on by his son when he joined the Army Air Corps. His job in the service was as physician and surgeon, just as Ephraim had been during the Civil War. Charles began practicing in the Hobbie/Wapwallopen area in 1903 where he later became well known for charging only fifty cents for an office visit. He had a wife named Verna Caroline Lloyd, and with her, fathered one child, Frederick LaMotte Santee.

Frederick was born 17 September 1906 in Wapwallopen, Pennsylvania and could read English and German at age three and then went on to learn Latin by studying Ephraim's old grammar books. Young Frederick became so fluent in Latin that when he was only eight years old, he wrote a translation of Caesar's *Gallic War* and then retranslated it to compare his prose with the original text. These early experiences with language inspired Frederick to want to become a Latin professor, and this became his life's ambition. Apparently foreign languages weren't his only strong suit. In

100

an interview with the *Gettysburg Star and Sentinel*, Santee's classmates claimed he was "a budding 'Babe' Ruth, whose heavy hitting had won more than one game for his team."

At the age of six, Santee knew as much Latin as the average college sophomore, but he suffered the common fate of gifted children in that his teacher didn't realize his advanced ability to read and comprehend not only the English language, but other languages as well. One day, his teacher was paying a visit to his father's medical office and noticed the young boy reading a newspaper and shortly thereafter, Frederick was promoted to the fourth grade.

Despite entering high school at the age of nine, Frederick wasn't a typical bookworm. He was very manly, and wanted to be a baseball player in the hopes that girls would like him better. During his summers, he helped build River Street, the small road that runs along the Susquehanna. However, his intellect was never doubted by anyone in his hometown. Townsfolk would frequently ask him questions about a book they might have read, and young Frederick would be able to recite the page that held the answer to their question.

In 1920, at the tender age of thirteen, Frederick was accepted to Harvard University in Boston. Reverend Clark Heller, a pastor of the Fairfield Reformed church and friend to Frederick, aided Santee in the admissions process through his contacts at Harvard. Papers around the nation carried news of his amazing achievement. The *Scranton Times* reported the story on September 11th of that year.

> Frederick Santee, 13, Wapwallopen, son of Dr. and Mrs. Santee has matriculated for the regular course in Harvard University. He is the youngest ever to enter as a candidate for degree. The boy has been unusual since his first day in school…

Of those years in Boston, Frederick later wrote: "I am the youngest member of the Class, probably the least successful,

Figure 31. Frederick Santee at age 17, just prior to his graduation from Harvard.

and possibly the only one who has never revisited Harvard. Perhaps these facts, on which my claim to uniqueness is based, are somehow interrelated." He spent summers working at a farm near Wapwallopen, but kept his own apartment (paid for by his parents) while at college. Santee excelled at Harvard; during his junior year he won the Bowdoin prize for excellence in Greek for his translation of ancient manuscripts, and also received acclaim for his Latin verses.

In fact, Frederick claims that the only valuable skill he received at Harvard was the ability to write Latin. For years after he left the University, Frederick corresponded in Latin with his old professor, E. K. Rand. It was here, in Boston, that his English professor, George L. Kittredge, first introduced him to the occult. Kittredge is perhaps best known for his work with Shakespearian literature and his important historical book *Witchcraft in Old New England*.

Frederick graduated from Harvard with an A.B. *magna cum laude* in 1924. After leaving Harvard, he and his mother traveled through Europe and the 18-year-old boy enrolled in the fall semester at Oxford as a classics major pursuing a B.A. This enrollment also garnered national media attention. The Elyria, Ohio *Chronicle Telegram* story on Santee reads:

> Frederick L. Santee, a Pennsylvania boy, entered Harvard at 13, and was graduated at 17. This fall he will go to Oxford in England. Some mothers and fathers will say that they are glad their son is not like that. They will say Frederick Santee is abnormal. They will expect to see him have brain fever or die young. As a matter of fact he simply illustrates the possibilities of the human intellect. He is what many other boys, some day, will be like...

While in England, he was inducted into numerous intellectual societies and became acquainted with W.B. Yeats at a branch of Alpha et Omega. Here, Frederick names his main influence in the occult as Professor Brabbart, his philosophy teacher at Oxford.

During Santee's time in London, the "modern witchcraft" movement was in full swing in Europe and he met several well-known witchcraft practitioners including Aleister Crowley and Israel Regarde. Contact with these influential and powerful members of European covens tantalized his mind, which had no doubt become jaded from years and years of study. Santee learned about the pagan religions, their rituals and beliefs from his new friends, and he was eventually inducted into the Hermetic Order of the Golden Dawn, a mysterious "magickal system" based on Freemasonry, Egyptian magic and other ancient traditions. With the help of Brabbart, he also became a member of the Theosophical Society of England.

After earning his B.A. and M.A. at Oxford, Frederick traveled to Germany and attended the University of Berlin in 1928. Here, in prewar Germany, occult practices thrived among the disenfranchised population. Will Schaber, a member of the press from the Weimar era recalls the climate in the book

Explaining Hitler. "It was a time when you had healers, seers, prophets emerging all over the countryside ... everyone was searching for a *Heiland* [healer/holy man]." In my correspondence with her, Lady Phoebe said, "Europeans wanted to be guided by him [Santee]."

Santee was drawn into this environment and his interest in the occult solidified upon meeting Arnold Reinman, the High Priest of a Wicca coven thirty miles outside Berlin. This lends some credibility to Frederick's claim that he was a homeopathic doctor to Adolph Hitler. It is well known that Hitler was interested not only in the occult, but also in alternative medicines, especially after the death of his mother. Hitler's mother, Klara, died in 1907 after enduring several months of ineffective, painful treatments to cure her breast cancer.

Dr. Bloch, her attending physician, applied extreme overdoses of iodoform, a disinfectant chemical that burns the skin, to Hitler's mother's tumor. The doctor remarked that during his treatments of Klara, her sufferings "seemed to torture her son. An anguished grimace would come over him whenever he saw pain contract her face." Given these circumstances, it does not seem improbable that Hitler would seek out practitioners of homeopathic medicine, Frederick Santee possibly being one of them.

In 1928, Frederick married Edith Rundle of Allentown, Pennsylvania. The marriage was an unusual affair, as was their entire relationship. More than twice his age, Edith and Santee had been little more than acquaintances when she invited him to follow her down to the county court house to "help with some paperwork." Being a well-mannered young man, he didn't stop to argue when she asked him to sign some papers in the presence of the county clerk. Directly after his signing, the clerk asked Santee when the wedding would occur. After responding with a puzzled look, Frederick was promptly informed that he had just signed a marriage certificate, and he and Edith were now married. If only the clerk had spoken a moment earlier, he could have prevented a most unpleasant and short-lived marriage.

While the story of the shanghaied husband is somewhat difficult to swallow, this is how Santee would recount his disastrous first marriage to friends in later years. Edith was supposedly not in her right mind, having suffered from bouts of schizophrenia for most of her life. Frederick said that he only stayed with her out of consideration and because he felt it was his duty to remain true to his commitment, even though he had pledged it unknowingly. Two years later, while he was still in Berlin, they adopted their only child, a daughter named Ruth.

During his time in Berlin, Santee traveled to the Middle East and in Egypt he met with multiple coven leaders. These early days abroad gave Frederick extensive background in occult practices and he learned a great deal from all the occultists he met. After leaving Berlin with a Ph.D, Santee began post-doctoral studies at the American Academy of Rome where he was a Sheldon Fellow and spent his time studiously, coming into occasional contact with coven members in Italy.

For six years, beginning in 1930, Santee was employed as a classics scholar, teaching at Lehigh, Temple, Vanderbilt, and Harvard Universities. All of these positions were held without tenure and usually Frederick was employed for only a short time, doing most of his teaching at Lehigh and Vanderbilt. Although he was happy with his position as a classics professor, Santee had difficulties with the political climate surrounding the universities he taught at. His position as an avowed socialist prevented him from receiving tenure and alienated him from the faculty and administration. "Surrounded constantly by a few devoted students," Santee says in his Harvard Yearbook autobiography, "I did my real teaching extra-curricular."

Frederick lost his teaching job during the Great Depression and in 1936 enrolled in the medical program at Johns Hopkins University at the urging of his father. He earned his MD in 1938 and immediately accepted a teaching position at

Kenyon College where he played a small part, for four years, in the humanistic revival that was taking place there.

During this time, Edith became more and more unstable as her schizophrenia reached uncontrollable levels. She was obsessed with the idea that Santee was having an affair with one of his female students, and could frequently be found at the university nearing an emotional breakdown. Edith's erratic behavior reached an all-time high when she began stalking through the campus grounds with an ax, intent on killing Frederick. In 1942, when he could finally take no more, Santee divorced Edith and married Betty Addis, of Cumberland, Maryland. Betty was more compatible with Frederick's personality. She was an accomplished poet and many of her works were later published. With Betty, Santee found a fellow intellectual and someone who could appreciate his incredible genius as well as his love of language.

At the dawn of WWII, a war that he vehemently opposed, Frederick was drafted into the US Navy Medical

Figure 33. Frederick Santee at age 43, looking like an average young professional.

Corps and promptly shipped off to the South Pacific where he bounced around for two years. This time spent constantly traveling from place to place while trying to support his new wife as well as his ex-wife left him heavily in debt. After his time in the South Pacific ended, Frederick finished his service at a shore command in Arkansas where he wrote a book of poems called *Sawdust and Tomatoes*.

When WWII was over in 1945, inflation, coupled with the needs of his family, forced Santee to give up his dream of being a college professor and he began practicing medicine. The doctor started working at a medical office in Baltimore, Maryland, but found the low-income area exceedingly unappealing and dreary. A failed partnership and losing his position as a professor at Johns Hopkins caused him increased financial hardship and Frederick decided to return to Wapwallopen to set up a private medical practice. "I recognize that money is my only aim in life as it should have been from the start," Santee wrote in 1950.

This was the low point of his life. Unable to make it in the "real world," this man who had left his hometown as a genius of unparalleled ability was forced to return and engage in a profession that was wholly unappealing to his lofty intellectual nature. Back in Wapwallopen, in the middle of nowhere, little stimulation was available for his fertile mind and Frederick Santee cannot be blamed for returning to his occult activities.

Upon his return to the tiny Pennsylvania hamlet, Frederick assisted with his father's medical practice. Sometime during 1956, his first year back in Wapwallopen, Frederick met Janie, a woman that he had hired as a nurse to work in his medical office. This woman would become his head nurse and eventually leader of the coven when he passed away.

When Santee's father died on 17 April 1963, he took over the office in his newly inherited home at 5 River Street. His wife Betty had died the year before, and their daughter Ruth had moved out long ago and was now with her second husband.

At this time, he employed two nurses, including Janie, and four office girls that worked part time and were young and attractive. Around 1963, Frederick began writing a column for the local newspaper called "The County Doctor," while Janie wrote a column titled "The Witches' Kettle."

In 1967 Frederick, Janie and the rest of the office staff were initiated into the New Forest Wicca lineage by the world-renowned High Priestess Sybil Leek, and with her help formed the Coven of the Catta (cat) in Wapwallopen. Together they laid the charter for the coven and Frederick became the High Priest while Janie was the High Priestess. In addition to their positions in the new coven, both received names to be used by fellow coven members. Santee was called Merlin and Janie was called Lady Phoebe.

Their sect honored the virtues of beauty, order and harmony and kept rituals in tune with the earth and aural energies. According to the Catta bylaws, a female is supposed to assume the role of leader to the coven members, however, the coven pushed Frederick to take the lead and he did until the end of his life. Originally, the entire coven gathered in the basement of Santee's house, but they eventually moved their meetings to the large book house on his property.

Santee had a massive library consisting of over 50,000 books with varying subject matter including biography, history, occultism, religion, medicine and philosophy. Some of the books in his collection were from as far back as the 15th century and a few were self-published texts. In 1979, one year before his death, Frederick penned his most successful book, a Faustian drama called *The Devil's Wager*. This play revisited the classic struggle between God and Satan over the soul of a single man.

In his book, the character of Faust is called Henry Stoddard and is described as "M.A. (Oxon), Ph.D. (Heidelberg), LL.D (Harvard), MD (Johns Hopkins)"; obviously representing Santee. There are other characters based on his life, three of which are tributes to his fellow coven members. The character

Miss Williams, and schoolgirls Edna and Jane, are three such examples. *The Devil's Wager* was written a year before Santee died and typifies his own struggle to realize his dream of being a college professor. It also deals with his early struggle to choose between mainstream religion and the Pagan rituals that had become so dear to him.

This book, along with another 50,000, was housed in the book house his father built as a practical way to store their combined literary collections. Some of the books were from the 17th century. The building also served as a place where quiet, comfortable study could occur, as the text of his will reads:

> The library is a cement block, one story building built piecemeal in a slab. It has a built-up roof, steel window frames, steel doors, dropped ceiling with recessed lighting and dry wall partitions inside. It was originally built about 1956 with an addition put on in 1960. The building is partially insulated and heated by electric heat. One section with semi-living conditions has a stone fireplace. There is one vault-type room and a small bathroom.

Figure 34. The book house adjacent to Dr. Santee's house.

Figure 35. Dr. Frederick Santee shortly before his death.

The Coven of the Catta continued practicing their Wiccan rituals, celebrating the cycles of the seasons throughout the seventies, reaching a peak membership of fifty people. Their activities no doubt frightened the locals and many formulated negative opinions about Dr. Santee and his coven. Of course, to small-town Christian people, any pagan religion would be considered evil and eventually rumors began to circulate, but these did not appear to hurt Santee's medical practice. His friendly nature coupled with an open-door policy, allowing the townspeople to enter his office and library at will, dispelled most of their serious fears.

Frederick always considered himself a teacher, and in that respect, he instructed many people in the ways of Wicca. He did believe in God, but was disenfranchised with organized religion, having declared in 1950, "In religion, I lean towards Anglo-Catholicism, am a member of no church." Santee's lack of faith in organized religion, coupled with the occult influences of his European travels caused him to begin practicing Wicca. His love of cats served as the basis for the coven's totem and upon his death in 1980, he left over $1,000 to various cat shelters. When a fire (allegedly started by prejudiced local teenagers) damaged the book house in 1977, one unfortunate feline was burned alive and its outline was permanently scorched on the concrete floor. That fire destroyed most of Santee's book collection, then valued at nearly $500,000. Upon inspecting the remains of his beloved library, the doctor remarked, "It's like seeing a lifetime fall in and crash around you."

Santee's obituary, posted in the local newspaper on 12 April 1980, was half a page long and taken almost entirely from the biography on the dust jacket of *The Devil's Wager*. According to his will, Janie inherited his house and most of his estate, which was valued at just over $200,000. She assumed leadership of the coven and continued practicing Wicca in Wapwallopen, occasionally bringing in new members from other areas of the state until old age forced her into retirement and her distant niece took control of the house at 5 River Street. Janie's niece is neither affiliated with the coven nor a practitioner of Wicca and the two are currently estranged.

The remaining members of the Coven of the Catta are mostly in Harrisburg, Pennsylvania, and they have formed a tight-knit group of witches dedicated to Wicca and preserving the traditions of Santee's original coven. Two of the founding witches live near Wapwallopen and still regularly visit the grave of their beloved High Priest. Following Dr. Santee's death, a variety of colorful urban legends sprang up about his activities as a witchcraft practitioner. As the years went on, and stories were told and retold, the level of evil and dangerousness of the coven increased.

Most of the older residents of Wapwallopen, those who really knew him and his family, firmly believe he was a good man and a wonderful doctor. Although, sometimes when you walk down River Street on a brisk fall day as the cool air blows off of the Susquehanna River, you can almost hear the whispers of the townspeople when you stop in front of house number 5. Some say the ghost of the doctor still haunts the place to this day, while others say he never haunted it at all.

Figure 36. Dr. Santee with Alice, one of his nurses.

This picture is perfect evidence of the fun, playful nature that Frederick Santee showed to those closest to him.

Courtesy M. Monroe.

112

How pleasant to know the good doctor
    Who writes all this horrible stuff;
Some call him a scoundrel and rotter,
    But a few think him pleasant enough.

His mind is abstract and fastidious,
    His nose is remarkably big;
Were he only a little less hideous,
    You would say he resembles a pig.

When he changes from far specs to near specs
    The children are frightened and cry,
And their mothers shout, "Hey! Don't you dare hex
    Poor Sam with your terrible eye!"

He has many friends, layman and clerical,
    He sleeps every night with his cats,
His body is perfectly spherical,
    His office girls never wear flats.

He is silent with people who talk a lot,
    He won't look at women in slacks,
His favorite flavor is chocolate,
    He rails at inflation and tax.

He hides in the depths of the cellar
    While his patients call down through the flue,
'Come out of that cellar, you yeller,
    You yeller old lazy bones you!'

He reads, but cannot speak, Spanish,
    He still prefers women to men;
Ere the days of your pilgrimage vanish,
    He hopes you will see him again.

A poem by Dr. Frederick Santee, about himself.

CHAPTER 5

The Mad Gasser of Botetourt County

Botetourt County, Virginia is dominated by forests and flanked by the Blue Ridge Mountains on the east. Botetourt's denizens were mostly farmers in 1933, but today, developers are changing the landscape by building housing for Roanoke's business class. The sleepy hamlet of Fincastle, located in the south-center of the County, served as "town" for the farming community, although now most of the local businesses have moved into neighboring Roanoke.

On the evening of December 22, 1933 a mysterious figure stepped from the shadows and attacked the residents of a rural farmhouse with an as-yet-undetermined substance which caused the afflicted persons much pain and discomfort. This figure would later become known as the Mad Gasser. The Gasser's most famous attacks actually occurred eleven years later in the town of Mattoon, Illinois, and it is that case which has received the majority of the publicity, with the Botetourt gassings usually occupying a little more than a footnote. However, when I first looked at the Mattoon and Botetourt gassings, I was intrigued because of their similarities, and it would appear that the same person or persons was clearly responsible for both attacks.

If we are to solve the mystery of the Mad Gasser, we must endeavor to piece together why someone would want to start gassing people in the first place, and in order to do that, we must revisit and focus on the first series of attacks that occurred in Botetourt County, Virginia. In attempting to determine what would drive a person to attack others with noxious gas, we have to look at several factors.

- What does the similarity of the victims tell us about who would want to hurt them?
- What is the significance of using gas as a weapon?
- Why were the police unable to identify the Gasser?

To conduct an in-depth investigation into this case, it was necessary for me to spend some time in Botetourt County. I traveled the back roads, ate in the restaurants, and talked to people whose families have lived in the area for generations. It's ironic that the majority of people I interviewed had no idea what a Mad Gasser was, and were totally oblivious to the fact that the 1933 attacks were their county's claim to paranormal fame. Perhaps this is because it was so long ago, and many of the victims were later made to feel foolish by the sheriff's department and the newspapers, which eventually attributed the gas attacks to mass hysteria.

In order to understand the dynamics of the gas attacks, we will first look at the evidence from each case, and then put together a theory that fits the available data. Bearing the facts of the evidence in mind, we shall proceed to elaborate on the victim's testimonials and put the mystery of the Mad Gasser to rest once and for all. I have developed not one, but three conflicting theories concerning the gas attacks and only one of them can be the truth. I will encourage the reader to choose which theory best fits the facts.

116

THE FACTS

- In several attacks, the heel print of a woman's shoe or boot was found.
- A 1933 Chevrolet with a man and a woman inside was seen in at least two cases.
- One victim reported four men running into the Blue Ridge Mountains.
- Victims reported hearing several voices outside their window.
- The gas smelled and tasted sickly sweet.
- The gas caused vomiting, facial swelling, nausea, numbness, restricted breathing, eye irritation, and in one case, convulsions.
- The victims were mostly farmers and their families.
- A residue of sulfur, arsenic, and mineral oil was found at the scene of one attack.

THE GAS

In his book, *The Mad Gasser of Mattoon*, author and high school chemistry teacher Scott Maruna deduced that the gas used by the Gasser was the chemical Nitromethane in liquid form which was sprayed into the victim's rooms. The inhalation of the vapors from the spray caused their symptoms. I concur with his deduction that an aromatic hydrocarbon is responsible for the attacks; however, I do not believe that Nitromethane was used in the Botetourt gassings.

What is an aromatic hydrocarbon? I asked myself the same question while I was working onboard the USS *Kearsarge* (LHD-3). One day, while walking down the passage way, I was nearly overcome by a strong sweet-smelling vapor. I later found out that this was the result of my fellow sailors applying a fresh coat of PRC, a chemical sealant which resembles plastic and is the standard floor coating on U.S. Navy ships. The smell lingered on my mind, and eventually it hit me that it was the same odor reported by victims of the Mad Gasser.

At my first opportunity, I found a can of the PRC chemical and carefully read the warnings on the label. It stated that aromatic hydrocarbons emit carcinogenic vapors and long term exposure will result in death. A list of short term exposure symptoms included dizziness, nausea, headache, and respiratory failure. I realized that the Mad Gasser had obviously used something very similar to the chemical compound I had been exposed to.

Armed with this knowledge, I began researching aromatic hydrocarbons. It was only a matter of identifying all the aromatic hydrocarbons in existence, and then narrowing them down to ones that fit the physical description of the liquid found at the two attacks, and a chemical to which the Gasser might have had access. The most commonplace aromatic hydrocarbons I found were in various industries; however the industrial hydrocarbon which best fits the description of the substance used in the gassing attacks was creosote.

Creosote is most widely used as a wood preservative, particularly for coating telephone poles. It is a dark yellow oily liquid and has a smoky or sweet odor. The vapors are strong and even brief exposure causes rapid illness and all the symptoms attributed to aromatic hydrocarbons. Creosote would be very easy to come by, especially for someone working in the lumber or coal industry, both of which were fairly common in Botetourt County. It would have been a simple matter of leaving work each day with a small container of creosote and then leaving a cloth soaked in the liquid near the open window of a victim. The vapors might take several minutes to fill the room, giving the Gasser plenty of time to hide in the shadows. Even if creosote was not the actual substance used, the same vapor-releasing tactic might be used for any aromatic hydrocarbon commonly found in industrial use.

There is another possible substance which fits all the reported symptoms and ties in nicely with some of the victim's stories. The poison may have been common insecticide; a simplistic answer, yes, but sometimes the simplest answer is the best. There are several compelling factors which suggest that the Mad Gasser used insecticide in the 1933 attacks. Symptoms of overexposure to insecticide are nearly identical to those reported by the victims, and many insecticides have a strong sweet odor. In the attack on J.G. Shafer a yellow oily liquid was found in the snow outside the house, which was determined to consist of arsenic, sulfur, and mineral oil, all ingredients of insecticide.

One attack, which was considered by investigators to be a hoax, actually involved insecticide. A woman was startled when a bottle of liquid flew through the window of her house. The police determined that the bottle contained insecticide and the attack had been the result of a copycat teenager pulling a prank. What is to stop us from believing that the entire series of gassings were nothing more than a teenage prank gone horribly out of control? These two cases were the only two to ever yield a sample of the substance, yet in neither was laboratory analysis taken seriously by police at the time. They just assumed that the gas must be something more mysterious than common insecticide.

It is perfectly reasonable to believe that insecticide was used in the Botetourt County gas attacks. In the agricultural community, every farmer in the County would have had a supply of insecticide for use on their crops. It is more than possible that the teenage children of one of these farmers decided to start a series of pranks and used their father's insecticide. The method of delivery could be varied, from a rag soaked in the chemical to a perfume sprayer, and still have the desired effect.

Let us step away from the most probable and onto the unlikely. The Mad Gasser may have been using a military-grade chemical gas. Just how the Gasser would acquire any supply of this gas is unknown, unless the culprit was the military itself (this is addressed later). For the sake of argument, let's say the Gasser was able to use military chemical weapons to attack his victims. There are three types of chemical agent used by militaries in gas form.

- Choking Agent
  - Smell: New mown hay or green corn.
  - Symptoms: Coughing, choking, tightness of chest, nausea, headache, watery eyes, breathing discomfort, fatigue, death.

- Nerve Agent
  - Smell: Fruity smell or camphor odor.
  - Symptoms: Drooling, nausea, vomiting, difficulty breathing, convulsions, runny nose, muscular twitching, death.

- Blood Agent
  - Smell: In aerosol form, lasts only seconds to minutes.
  - Symptoms: Giddiness, headache, confusion, nausea, difficulty breathing, cramps, loss of consciousness, bluing of skin, death.

So there are several candidates for the mysterious gas within the military's chemical weapons stockpile. However, the primary purpose of chemical weapons is to incapacitate and kill. It is highly unlikely that someone who has been exposed to a military-grade nerve, choking, or blood agent would survive the attack if not immediately treated with an atropine/2-PAM chloride injection. If we believe that the Gasser was not acting at the behest of the United States military, then all of these options should be discounted. Otherwise, we should be led to believe that the gas attacks in both Botetourt County and Mattoon, Illinois were the work of military agents.

A MUNDANE EXPLANATION

Of the three theories that I have developed, this is the most mundane, and the most probable. It is highly likely that the Mad Gasser was acting out of anger and a desire for revenge. The victims are not directly related and most of them are farmers; although some have other jobs, they are not all employed by the same company, or in the same profession. Therefore, we can safely say that the Gasser's motivation was probably personal, and not professional. It is also interesting to note that on November 14, 1933, the Roanoke Fire Department responded to a record fourteen fire alarms in less than five hours. Based on this seldom-reported fact, we might be led to believe that the Gasser actually began as a Mad Arsonist, and when that proved to be too risky, he decided to get his revenge through other methods.

Diving into the lives of people I never knew who lived in a place I have only visited twice was not easy. The process of uncovering the minutiae of the lives of the victims is vital to developing a list of suspects. However, all there is to go on is newspaper reports, the stories of their grandchildren, and census data. There are downsides to all of this information. Newspaper reports do not tell the whole story, and in some cases actually reported incorrect information about the victims. Most of the descendants of the victims were never told about the gas attacks, and I have not been able to find a living witness. Fincastle resident Bob Willis wrote a series on the Mad Gasser attacks for the local paper, and was fortunate enough to interview a daughter of one of the victims. However, after reviewing the 1930 census, I determined that the girl in question had not been born, or was under three years of age at the time of the gassings, and therefore any story she told Willis would have been second-hand information.

The 1930 census has proved to be a valuable asset in my quest to get to know the residents of Botetourt County. Unfortunately, I had to wait some time to study it. The U.S.

Figure 37. The author meeting with Mad Gasser reporter and Fincastle local Bob Willis.

government keeps all census data under lock and key until seventy-two years after the census date in order to protect privacy. Once the census data was released to the public, I had to wait a further two years for it to be scanned and entered in database form on a public genealogy website so I could search it easily in my spare time. The 1930 census recorded address, education, family members, dates of birth and marriage, job status, occupation, and veteran status.

All of this information was vitally important to my research. Using the census, I determined that the victims were mostly farmers, and almost none of them were veterans. I was also able to "correct" some of the name misspellings found in the newspaper reports. For example, the man involved in the very first attack was reported as Cal Huffman, but his full name is Claude Huffman. The fourth victim, Homer Hylton is actually Daniel "Homer" Hylton, and the newspapers frequently misspelled the name of Hylton's neighbor, Emmit Lee. One extreme inconsistency was the existence or non-existence of Cal Huffman's daughter Alice, who was reported to have been severely afflicted by the first gas attack (which consisted of three attacks on the same house in one night).

I have been unable to prove that Huffman actually had a daughter named Alice. However, his neighbor and landlord, Kent Henderson, who arrived at the Huffman household with his son shortly after the first attack, had a girl living with him in 1930 named Alice Cronise, who was nineteen years old in 1933; the same age Huffman's non-existent daughter was reported to be. Here we have a case of gross misreporting on the part of the local press. The likely scenario is that after the first two attacks, Kent Henderson arrived at the Huffman home with his son and his niece, Alice. When the third gas attack occurred, Alice was in the house and therefore afflicted by the noxious fumes. Why the local paper would have reported her as being Huffman's daughter is beyond me. I considered that perhaps she was his daughter-in-law, but Huffman's eldest son was only thirteen in 1933, and unlikely to have been married to a nineteen-year-old girl. Also, Huffman's wife Nancy was born in 1902, making her twelve years old when Alice was born. I think we can safely say that Alice was not Cal Huffman's daughter.

The reason Alice's identity is so crucial is because she was the most afflicted of any of the gassing victims. *The Roanoke Times* reported that after inhaling the gas, she fell unconscious and had to be revived by a doctor who was on the scene. Whoever the Gasser was, he obviously had a grudge of some kind against the Huffman family. If Alice was indeed Cal's daughter, then perhaps the Gasser was an estranged lover who was seeking revenge on his love interest. However, if Alice lived down the road at Kent Henderson's house, then this scenario is not valid.

One scenario I have developed is centered on Alice Cronise. Perhaps she was an unruly teenager who was sent to live with her uncle, possibly in the hope that working on the farm would calm her restless demeanor. Kent Henderson had two sons, one of which was Alice's age. As three bored teens, they might have decided to start playing "pranks" on local people they didn't like. Perhaps they knew of a chemical (creosote or insecticide) which was readily available to one of them that had adverse effects to anyone who breathed in the vapors. The three teens began their mischief by gassing Henderson's tenant who lived down the road, which was easily accessible by foot; this was one of the cases where no car was reported at the scene.

After attacking the Huffman's twice and getting away with it, they were probably surprised when Cal asked Kent Henderson to come to his house and help guard against another gas attack. Kent's son Ashby and niece Alice both went along to "help" keep an eye out for suspicious prowlers. While the two teens were in the house, their third gassing accomplice, Grover Henderson, released another dose of the toxic substance into the house. It is reported that Ashby Henderson was outside with Cal when the attack happened, although he was affected by the gas. If they were a party to the gassings, then they would've faked the symptoms, with Alice going the extra mile and pretending to be unconscious. Their status as victims would automatically absolve them from any guilt, even if they fell under suspicion at a later date.

A car was seen in connection with numerous attacks, but only in the later attacks which took place in rural areas. It would've been easy for the attackers to drive their car into town and park it in an out of the way place and then begin a series of gassings each night. The car that the Mad Gasser was frequently seen running towards or speeding away in was described as a 1933 Chevrolet. Based on this alone, we can rule out the possibility that the Gasser was some disaffected poor person. During the Great Depression, there was no poor rural farmer who could've afforded a brand new car. It very plausible that Kent Henderson, who owned the house the

Huffman's lived in, might've been wealthy enough to own a new car, and would've let his son take it out for a drive. Using this as their getaway vehicle, the three teens were free to gas anyone they chose.

The panic and publicity of their first attacks may have simply encouraged the teens to continue the gassings, finally stopping when they came too close to getting caught. This theory does fit the facts. A woman's heel print was found at the scene of the attacks, multiple people were noticed fleeing the scenes, and the apparent randomness of their victims indicates a small group of thrill-seeking young people. If no motive can be synthesized, then the gassings must be the result of either a deranged person or a mischief-maker. The fact that multiple people were apparently responsible for the gas attacks suggests that it could not have been the work of a deranged loner. Therefore, if the Mad Gasser was a local person, it must have been a small group of thrill-seeking teenagers attacking random targets, and ones from a family with access to a 1933 Chevrolet.

Figure 38. A WWI-era Lancer wearing a gas mask. Some researchers think the Gasser was a deranged veteran.

A MILITANT EXPLANATION

There is some evidence to suggest that the Mad Gasser was actually a member of the United States military. Local law enforcement's inability to capture the Gasser, or determine what substance was being used in the attacks suggests that the Gasser was operating with a high degree of sophistication, on par with Special Forces soldiers. It is well known that in the early days of chemical weapons development, the U.S. government took unsafe liberties with the American public. There are numerous accounts, which surfaced after the fact, of military units spraying civilian communities with chemical and biological weapons just to see what would happen. Unfortunately, this practice was not infrequent. There are at least twenty documented cases between 1941 and 1970 where the U.S. military deliberately contaminated civilians and military personnel who were unaware of what was being done to them.

Placed in context, the scenario does not seem implausible. Imagine that the U.S. Army Medical Research Institute for Infective Diseases (USAMRIID) conducts an experiment in 1933 in an isolated community to determine America's vulnerability to a chemical attack. Over the course of two months, victims are chosen at random and given small amounts of deadly gasses, most likely choking or nerve agents. The dosage is not enough to kill them, but enough to enable the military to gauge their reaction. After their experiment is complete, they move on and the reports simply stop. The lack of any viable suspects forces the police and newspapers to attribute the whole thing to mass hysteria. The experiment is then repeated eleven years later during WWII in Mattoon, Illinois; another isolated community that had no knowledge of the previous study.

There is also the possibility that the military wasn't using a chemical or biological weapon, but they may have been testing a new insecticide. Remember DDT and Agent Orange?

126

The active ingredients of DDT were first developed in 1873 by a German chemistry student, although it was not actually used as an insecticide until 1939. However, it was widely used by Allied troops to control insect-borne typhus in Europe. How could they have used it in populated areas without first conducting some experiments?

There is little hard evidence to support this theory, although if the military were truly the culprit, they would have left little evidence behind, and even if a secret soldier were to be caught red handed, the government would have ceased the project immediately and stopped those "in the know" from talking. Remember, 1933 was not like it is today; there was no Federation of American Scientists filled with whistle-blowers eager to expose the government's black box projects. Until the true composition of the gassing agent can be determined once and for all, which is now unlikely, the possibility of military involvement in the Botetourt gassings can only be speculated.

A MYSTERIOUS EXPLANATION

Leaving behind the restraints of reality, let us delve into the truly bizarre. Very few investigators have bothered to speculate on the possibility that the Mad Gasser's origins were from beyond the realm of our understanding. However, considering the authorities' inability to capture the Gasser or produce a viable suspect, we must think about a different suspect altogether.

If the Gasser was from another planet, or another dimension, or some fantastic creature with super powers, then there would have to be some evidence for this in the Botetourt attacks. When J.G. Shafer of Lithia was gassed, he found woman's shoe prints in the snow leading from his front porch to the barn behind his house, but there were no prints leading away from the barn. To where did the Gasser disappear? No one can answer this, but from this incident, and based on the fact that the police were unable to capture the culprit, we are led to believe that perhaps the Gasser did have powers beyond that of a normal human.

Perhaps the Gasser was a mutated human being, either through some freak laboratory accident which left him both superhuman and demented, or as a result of a birth defect. This laboratory accident could have been less accident and more experiment, resulting in an intentional physiological change and used for evil purposes. It is also possible that the Gasser was some form of alien life from another planet, although the reason such a visitor would want to expose humans to noxious gas is a separate question altogether.

A visitor representing an alien race might be interested in colonizing the planet Earth, but maybe our atmosphere isn't totally conducive to their race, and they have made plans to alter the chemical composition of the atmosphere to make it more livable to their species. Before going ahead with a massive project like that, the aliens would want to test the effects of the foreign atmosphere on humans to see what their reaction would be. The Gassers, as alien soldiers, may have been subjecting victims to small doses of gas with the same chemical makeup as their home planet's atmosphere. The human reaction to this chemical was negative, and the aliens realized that the entire planet would perish if they went ahead with the total atmospheric change, so the experiment stopped. Several years later, when the Mattoon gassings began, perhaps the aliens were testing a new form of gas, slightly "improved" from the old one that had been used in Botetourt County. This gas also failed, and the aliens were forced to begin a long term project of creating hybrid humans which would be able to live in the modified atmosphere.

I have also considered a less nefarious alien gas connection. It is possible that the alien creature was itself the source of the noxious fumes. No, I'm not suggesting it was burrito night on the spacecraft. Perhaps the chemical composition of the alien creatures is different from that of human beings, and as a result, their natural odor is more than repugnant. To a human, it is downright harmful. Believe it or not, there is some evidence to support this particular theory of alien body odor.

In 1996, NASA scientists announced that they had found evidence of life on Mars. This evidence came not in the form of a spaceship landing on the White House lawn, but from close examination of a meteorite that was found in Allen Hills, Antarctica. Meteorite ALH84001 was a piece of the planet Mars which had broken off and, with other fragments that have been found over the years, landed on the surface of the Earth. The team of NASA scientists determined that ALH84001 contained polycyclic aromatic hydrocarbons in the form of fossilized nanobacteria, bacteria which is not visible microscopically and smaller than any life on Earth. I mentioned earlier that the gas used in the Botetourt and Mattoon attacks was most likely an aromatic hydrocarbon of some kind, and therefore, it is logical to assume that a larger version of this alien life form is made of aromatic hydrocarbons and might be inadvertently responsible for the gas attacks.

Figure 39. Meteorite ALH840001. *Courtesy NASA.*

The theory that the Mad Gasser was an alien is a long shot, I know, and highly unlikely, but it does fall in the realm of extreme possibility. Of course, we are missing the one crucial piece of evidence which might lend some validation to this theory, and that is the presence of UFOs at the site of the gas attacks. The apparent fact that no UFOs were sighted would lead us to naturally assume that there were no aliens either.

CONCLUSIONS

The Botetourt gas attacks are one of the few paranormal mysteries which may be solved with only dedicated detective work. I am confident that with more research and investigation, I can finally unravel the riddle of the Mad Gasser and reveal his, her, or their identities. One promising idea I have is to compare the 1930 Botetourt County census with the 1940 Mattoon, Illinois census and simply pick out anyone who lived in Botetourt and then later moved to Mattoon. Obviously this person would be the primary suspect and would give me a specific individual on which to focus my efforts. Unfortunately, I will be unable to utilize this method until at least 2012 due to the U.S. government's seventy-two-year confidentiality period on all census data.

Barring the usage of the above method, it may never be possible to conclusively prove who the Mad Gasser of Botetourt County was. With the passage of time, we may never know what would compel a person or people to attack others with noxious gas. Perhaps they truly were mad, and that might be all the reason they require.

CHAPTER 6

The Gasser's First Victims

To find out what really happened in Botetourt County, Virginia back in 1933, we must journey through time and watch the thrilling night when the Mad Gasser first appeared. The following story is a work of fiction, based on the newspaper reports which were written during the time the gas attacks occurred.

It was a chilly winter night when Cal Huffman and his wife Nancy left the house of their friend Kent Henderson. The darkness had already descended over the treetops, and the stars were bright against the moonless, pale blue sky. Despite the luminescence of the stars, very little of the light permeated to the eyes of Mr. and Mrs. Huffman. The woods around them were dark. It was the kind of dark that people write poems about in the hopes of terrifying children. It was country dark, with no light seeping in from the city street lamps. Only the dim light from the stars above shone through the leafless branches over their heads.

A gentle breeze flowed around the couple as they began to walk down the country road that would take them from the Henderson residence to their own. Although the breeze that

Figure 40. The Blue Ridge Mountains, Botetourt County.

night was soft, combined with the already low December temperature, it made the journey home slightly uncomfortable. Nancy moved closer to her husband, hoping to share some of the warmth emanating from his body. She put her hand in the pocket of his heavy wool hunting jacket, the one with the leather patch on its shoulder to protect it from premature wear at the butt of a rifle. Here, her small hand stayed warmer than any other part of her body because it was the part of her closest to her husband.

The hooting of an owl could be heard in the distance, its large wings flapping through the dense thicket growing on both sides of the dirt road. Would he catch a mouse? Nancy wondered. It's late December, and there would be no insects to eat. How do predators stay alive during the barren season? Surely the owl could find at least one mouse a night to eat. Would that really be enough for such a large bird, only a single mouse a night? No, the owl must spend the entire hours of darkness searching for its prey, taking what it can get like a scavenger.

Suddenly, her husband stopped in his tracks. Something must be wrong, she thought, Cal isn't one to spook easily. Growing up on a farm, working from day to night, hunting for

132

extra food during the winter, Cal was accustomed to the woods and the out-of-doors. Having lived in the farmhouse deep in those woods, Cal was well aware of his surroundings, and as a practical man, his imagination was never prone to run wild.

Too anxious to say anything, Nancy simply stood in her tracks, her hand in her husband's pocket, waiting. The two of them stood silently in the middle of the road, Cal's arm around his wife's waist, listening to the night, feeling that something might be wrong. It felt like someone was watching them. Two nights ago, while Cal was walking back from the Henderson's house alone, he was sure he heard someone or something in the woods, following his steps. Several times, the big man stopped, only to have the cracking of dry branches and leaves stop with him.

At first, he though it was deer, but then as the sounds progressed and appeared to follow him, Cal became suspicious that a person was lurking in the darkness. A figure mixed in among the shadows of the leafless trees, trailing his movement down the country road for an unknown but probably nefarious reason.

Squinting his eyes, not wanting to alarm his wife, Cal peered into the darkness of the woods, seeing nothing. Two nights ago, there had at least been a quarter moon, allowing him to make out shapes and blobs in the thicket. Now, all he could see was darkness, pitch-blackness, nothing. Why would someone want to follow him home? It didn't make sense, but the idea of a prowler lurking through the darkness while his wife and daughter were home alone wasn't a very appealing thought, so Cal fixed his eyes on the road ahead and continued on, writing off the noises as deer.

The moment Cal turned back to the road, one of the unidentifiable blobs leapt out of the darkness and into his face. Nancy screamed, wrapping both hands around her husband, who, despite the grip of his wife, threw up his hands to protect his face from the unseen assailant. In a flash of wings and feathers, the owl swooped up across the road to the branch of a tree, looking back at his victims with large, all-seeing eyes. The couple stared angrily at the owl's eyes, illuminated by the starry sky.

A moment after, the large owl left his heightened perch to look for ground dwellers that were considerably easier to digest, and left the Huffmans to finish their walk unhindered. As the owl flew off into the night, they found the humor in the whole incident and laughed together before Cal kissed his wife on the lips to let her know everything was all right now.

Trying to escape the nighttime cold, they began walking quicker than usual and fifteen minutes later, they saw the warm glow of their farmhouse sitting back off the road. Moving past the trees that overshadowed the entrance to their driveway, the Huffmans approached their home, both glad to be off the country road and out of the deep darkness engulfing the steps behind them.

Only one light was on in the Huffman home that night. Alice, their twenty-year-old daughter was sitting in the living room reading a book about mathematics. Her eventual goal was to start attending Hollins College in Roanoke the coming fall. She wanted to get her teaching degree and be a schoolteacher. The elder Huffmans approved of the idea, and encouraged their only daughter's pursuits as best they could.

Alice worked as a storekeeper at Nannie's Market, the roadside store near their house. It was about an hour walk, but she could make it there in twenty minutes on her bike. The winter months aren't kind to a young girl riding a bike, so sometimes her father would take her to work in his car and the store's owner, Warren Nash would drive her home at night. Because today had been a Friday, Alice had been allowed to leave work early, and since it was a pleasant day, she had decided to walk herself home.

The sun was shining and there was no wind in the air, which was good because Alice hated the wind. It was a force that she couldn't control; Mother Nature spitting in her face, sometimes cold, sometimes warm, but always uncontrollable.

While in high school, Alice worked at the store part time, walking there when school was over and working for a few hours then making the long trip home to have dinner with her parents. Occasionally, someone she knew would stop and give her a ride, but more frequently, she was forced to walk home by herself.

That was when the wind was the worst. During the winter, by herself, the bitter cold wind screamed in her face, turning her cheeks and hands red and raw. There was no way to stop it. She could try walking backwards, but it was too clumsy and she inevitably went back to walking forwards shortly after trying. No matter how thickly her scarf was wrapped or how tightly she held her gloved hands, the wind always found a way into her clothes. It seemed to know how to find her skin, as if there were little holes in her outerwear that only the wind could see. And then when it made contact with skin, it would blow and blow and blow with all its terrible might. Such are the forces of Mother Nature, and they did not, at times, agree with Alice.

During her walk home today, she was especially thankful for the lack of wind and for the abundance of sun that was shining into her crystal brown eyes. They sparkled the way a baby's sparkle in the glow of a mother's love. Alice's eyes were like gemstones that no jeweler could set anywhere except within her sockets. And so, eyes sparkling, hair sticking out playfully from under the knit cap her mother had made for her, Alice proceeded down the country road to her house.

Nearly halfway home, she stopped to look at a brook that was running through the ice covering its surface. The slow running stream water flowed through holes in the ice like it was overflowing with life, eager to escape the confines God had placed it in. Don't worry, Alice thought, you'll be in the ocean soon enough, and then you'll never have to worry about being trapped beneath the ice ever again. It was a fun to imagine that the flowing brook water she was looking at right now would someday be in the ocean, a place she herself had never been to.

Kneeling down on the roadside to take a drink from the icy water, Alice suddenly became aware of a person watching her from the woods. Looking up, she clearly saw a woman dressed in black standing atop the ridge extending the length of the road. Startled by her unannounced visitor, Alice stood up and watched the woman watching her from a distance.

Having forgotten her manners, letting her curiosity get the better of her, Alice regained composure and decided to wave hello to the woman. Perhaps a greeting would put them on friendly terms and she'll have a walking companion, she thought. The woman on the ridge was not as cordial. After a minute of waving and shouting "Hello" loud enough so that she was certain the woman could hear her, Alice abandoned her attempts at friendship. It's an irregular thing to be standing on a ridge watching a person, and even more irregular to not respond when greeted; perhaps it was best for Alice to just continue on her way and let the strange woman go back to her business.

Drying off her hands on her pants, Alice looked up to the ridge once more and discovered that the strange woman had disappeared. No sound, not even a rustle of dry leaves, no trace and no proof that she had ever been there in the first place. Considering that she was delirious from drinking the creek water, Alice returned to the road and tried to put the whole incident from her mind. And so she kept walking the entire way home, occasionally looking over her shoulder to make sure the strange woman wasn't following her.

The mathematics book that lay on her lap now consumed Alice's thoughts as her parents unlocked the front door and entered the house. So transfixed was she with square roots, that Alice scarcely noticed her parents' arrival until their entrance was announced by the loud thud of the front door.

As Nancy and Cal removed their coats and hung them in the closet by the front door, Alice set her book aside, dog-earing the last page she had read. Her parents moved quickly into the living room, her father sliding closed the deadbolt, securing the door for the remainder of the evening. It was now nine-thirty, and after some casual conversation about their evening at Henderson's, Alice decided to retire to her bedroom while her parents stayed in the living room drinking apple cider and relaxing before going to bed themselves.

Alone in her bedroom, Alice slowly undressed and put on the slip that she would wear to bed. Last year, while at a sleepover with some of her girlfriends, Alice discovered that none of them wore pajamas to bed like she did. Instead, most of them wore their silk slips that were usually reserved for under dresses. It was even more interesting that some of them slept totally naked or stripped down to bra and panties. Eager to try a new experience and with the coaching of her friends, Alice spent that night sleeping naked in her sleeping bag on her friend's bedroom floor.

When asked the next day how she felt, Alice had to truthfully respond that her sleep had been rather restless and she found it difficult to get comfortable having no clothes on. So the next night, while back in her own bed, she tried sleeping in just her underwear, but the bra felt too constricting and left marks from the pressure of her body resting in the same spot the entire night. Later, she resorted to only panties, which also proved too uncomfortable to sleep in after wearing them all day. Finally, she attempted the most exotic of her options, and found it very tolerable.

The feeling of the silk against her naked body as she slept was exhilarating and comforting at the same time. It was soothing as she rolled around in her bed during the night, and regardless of the condition she was in when lying down to sleep, Alice always woke up feeling refreshed and invigorated, ready to face the day. Her slip was easily her favorite article of clothing. Alice laid her head down on her pillow and drifted off to sleep.

In the living room, her parents were quietly winding down from the events of the day. Their evening with Kent Henderson had been rather uneventful. Cal and Kent were friends from high school and had grown up next to each other, spending most of their time together as teenagers. Both men met and married their wives in the same month and each served as the other's best man. Where Cal was a farmer from a family of farmers, Kent worked for the county as a maintenance man.

During the Great War (as WWI was called in those days), because he was childless, Kent joined the war effort and was shipped off to France in 1917. At the conclusion of hostilities a year later, he returned home to find his wife gone. She found herself unable to remain faithful to her husband while he was so far away and left with a new husband for parts unknown. Kent was devastated by his loss. His wife was the only thing he wanted from the world, but her love had never run as deep as his did.

Upon returning from the war, the county gave its veterans civil service jobs for which they were qualified, so Kent became a maintenance worker, repairing telephone poles, patching roads and fixing the street lamps in Fincastle, the county seat. His job gave him enough to get by on, but not quite enough to truly prosper. Living by himself made it a little easier on finances, but much harder on a man who had loved and lost.

That particular night, the Huffmans were dropping by to play cards and talk about the weather with Kent. Nancy wished Mr. Henderson would hurry up and find a Mrs. Henderson or at least a girlfriend so she would have someone to talk to while he and Cal were reminiscing about old times. It would also bring Kent out of the mourning phase he seemed to have been in ever since he got back from the war.

Now alone in their living room, Nancy sat in a large chair by the window working on her needlepoint while Cal read *Farmer's World* magazine, dozing on the couch. Looking at the clock, she noted it was 10:05, almost time for bed, and returned to her delicate tapestry. It was of a cat playing with a ball of twine, and she intended to use real twine to sew the ball. Although it would be difficult to force the thick thread through the tiny needlepoint holes, Nancy was confident this would set the tapestry apart from all her others.

Without warning, she was overcome by the strong smell of gas. Fearing the worst, she dropped her needlepoint and shook her husband from his groggy half-asleep state. Cal immediately smelled the gas and left Nancy in the living room while he checked the stove in the kitchen. The smell of gas was nonexistent as soon as he left the living room, and upon checking the stove, Cal was shocked to find the pilot light still on. After a cursory examination of the wall connection, he was satisfied that nothing was wrong with the stove.

Returning to the living room, Nancy was lying on the couch, her hand resting on her head, complaining that she was nauseous. The gas had completely dissipated from the room, and after peeking in his daughter's room to make sure there was no gas smell, Cal quietly closed the door and returned to his wife's side with a glass of water. By this time, Nancy was already feeling a little better, but still light-headed. She took the water her husband gave her and sat up on the couch to drink it.

There was no telling where the strange gas had come from and only after turning the problem over in their minds did they jointly discovered that the window by Nancy's chair was slightly ajar. It was late December and bitterly cold outside, so both husband and wife agreed that they hadn't opened the window that night. Cal promptly closed it and retrieved his flashlight from the hall closet.

Checking once more on Nancy to ensure her symptoms of exposure to the gas were subsiding, he went outside, locking the door behind him. There was no snow on the ground, but Cal had a sneaking suspicion that whoever had been watching him in the woods two nights ago was back, and they were playing some kind of a prank on his family. This wasn't right, it just wasn't right to mess with a man's family, especially one as terrific as Cal's.

Outside, the wind had picked up and was blowing furiously against the house sending dry leaves and small broken branches flying through the air. It was the kind of wind Alice would have hated. Fortunately, she was tucked safely in her warm bed and it was her father who had the unpleasant task of getting to the bottom of this late-night mystery.

Cal's flashlight pierced the darkness but didn't seem to shine quite far enough for his comfort. While he was a large man, made strong by years and years of farm labor, it didn't suit Cal to be out in the pitch darkness in the middle of the night with a mysterious stranger. It was all the more unsettling to think that this person had potentially been following him only a few nights before, but for what reason?

The bottom of the window was situated directly above Cal's chest. He could see his wife inside, lying on the couch, sipping her water. If someone had been out here, they would've been able to watch the people inside and choose the moment to strike with leisure. That thought, more than any other, made his skin crawl. There had been reports of prowlers or peeping Tom's in the city, but never out here in the country. Cal believed that the country was filled with mostly good people, but the city had so many people that a good percentage of them were bound to be prone to bad things.

Carefully inspecting the windowsill with his flashlight, Cal found what looked like scrapes from a Flathead screwdriver. The window was unlocked, and it would've been easy to pry it open with a flat chisel or some other tool. He tried to lift the window up with just his hands and found it difficult, but possible. In the interest of not accidentally breaking the pane of glass, Cal abandoned his experiments and returned to the house, letting himself in with his key.

By this time, Nancy had sufficiently recovered and her husband helped her into the bedroom. When she was beneath the covers, Cal left the bedroom and went to the couch in the living room where he sat watching the window. Sitting on the couch, he turned the events of the evening over in his mind, wondering who could be responsible for such a bizarre act.

While questions ran through his mind, Cal slowly drifted off to sleep, his head resting comfortably on the back of the couch.

Shortly after Cal Huffman drifted off to sleep, the bedroom his wife was sleeping in began to fill with the same gas that had earlier been in the living room. Nancy was stirred awake and found herself gasping for air. The smell of the gas also woke Cal from his peaceful slumber on the couch and he quickly pulled his wife from the bedroom and brought her into the living room. She was gasping and coughing but appeared to be all right aside from that.

After ensuring that Nancy was fine and comfortable, Cal entered the bedroom and found there to be no trace of the noxious fumes that filled the air only a moment before. He quickly inspected the two windows and found them both locked with the glass intact. The gasser had obviously returned, but his modus operandi had changed slightly and he was now leaving no clues. If not through the window, then how? Due to the strangeness of it all, Cal was in no mood to play games. He went to the kitchen and called the county sheriff.

Deputy sheriff Oscar Lemon was standing the night shift in the Fincastle sheriff's office. The office was conveniently located between the county courthouse and the county jail with an attorney's office off to the right. The entire legal procedure from arrest to imprisonment could be conducted within the confines of the same small-town block. Across the street was Van's Restaurant and Pub, where Oscar had eaten his dinner earlier that evening. Of course, because he was on the night shift, it was more like his breakfast, but it suited him none the less.

A lean man with angular facial features, Oscar had a second job as an interior/exterior painter. He mostly did houses and office buildings, but occasionally he picked up other odd jobs around the town. That was how he got the job as a deputy sheriff, by painting. Four years ago he was working on the county clerk's office (an annex of the courthouse) when he overheard the county supervisor complaining that they were shorthanded and needed more deputy sheriffs. While he never kept steady jobs, Oscar spoke up and pending completion of a two-month training and instruction period, he was hired on the spot.

Here he was thirty-two years old and had no serious complaints about his life. He didn't have a girlfriend, though that would've been nice. And he wasn't as handsome as some men his age were, but bearing no further responsibilities other than those to himself, he was traveling through life freely and setting his own pace. There would be time to get married and have children later, he thought. Maybe when he had saved up enough money, and owned a house, would be the time to start searching out prospective brides.

Extinguishing a cigarette in the ashtray on his cluttered desk, Oscar picked up the ringing phone. Usually he sat at Sheriff Mundy's desk. It was the biggest and had the most comfortable chair, which was only fitting for a county sheriff. Tonight, however, he had to file a series of receipts that had come in from the county clerk's office earlier that day. Paperwork was the one part of the job Oscar hated, but it came with a paycheck, so he didn't complain too loudly.

The man on the line was Cal Huffman, sounding frantic, trying to describe the attacks his family had been suffering at the hands of a shadowy assailant. Oscar couldn't quite make out what Cal was trying to tell him over the phone, but he agreed to take a drive over to his house and see to the problem. Cal seemed satisfied with that and hung up the phone.

Finishing the last of the receipts, Deputy Sheriff Lemon started his patrol car and let it warm up before leaving the station. It was a cold night, and the 1932 Ford wouldn't turn over until the third try. Letting the engine idle for a few minutes while locking the doors, Oscar got in the patrol car and began the short drive to Haymakertown where Huffman lived.

Upon leaving the streetlights and plunging into the country darkness, Oscar became concerned about deer. Sheriff Mundy had banged up the other patrol car while responding to a late-night call in the woods. Didn't even see it coming, he said. Keeping the high beams on, Oscar proceeded with caution, driving at safe speeds the entire trip. He had no idea what would be waiting for him at the Huffman residence.

The scene as he pulled up the driveway off Haymakertown Road was one of surprise, as all the lights in the one-story house were turned on, including the outside porch light. Turning off the engine and putting on his brown felt sheriff's hat, Oscar stepped from his patrol car up to the stairs and knocked on the door. If the sight of a house full of lights had surprised Deputy Lemon, the sight in the living room downright shocked him.

All three members of the Huffman family seemed to be losing their minds. After closing the door behind him, Cal immediately tried explaining his story in rambling fragments, skipping from one part to another. Mrs. Huffman was doing the same, although she was speaking rather loudly while lying on the couch, still recovering from her earlier attack. Young Alice seemed to be the only one who had retained her sanity. Although she was the only one not speaking, she seemed to have no idea what was going on.

Her parents had woken her after the second gas attack and told her to get dressed because someone from the sheriff's office was coming to have a look at the place. They didn't explain anything about what had happened, only that she had to stay with the family in the living room until the sheriff came out. Not being one to question her parent's motives, Alice obeyed and now sat quietly with her mother on the couch wearing a bathrobe over her slip and red socks on her feet.

She made her mother tea while waiting for Deputy Lemon to arrive, and was alarmed that her father insisted she not use the stove. After some discussion on the impossibility of boiling water without heat, Cal changed his mind and instead warned her to be extremely careful while turning it on, and to make sure the pilot light didn't go out when she was finished.

The cup of lukewarm earl gray tea was resting on the floor in its saucer while Nancy tried desperately to have her side of the story told. Oscar finally got both elder Huffmans to calm down and speak to him rationally, and listened as first Nancy and then Cal told their versions of the attack. Alice listened in awe to their tales, in total disbelief that they had let her sleep though the excitement, and partly jealous that she didn't have a story of her own to tell.

Deputy Lemon was in a state of disbelief himself as he took down their statements in his notebook, making only cursory notes, things to put in the report and tell the sheriff about in the morning. Listening more than writing, Oscar was convinced that there was some kind of misunderstanding prevailing between husband and wife, and the details of the attack were getting skewed. It was his understanding that someone had entered their house through a window and turned on the gas on the stove, causing Mrs. Huffman to become ill.

Only after Cal urged Deputy Lemon outside to look at the window was anything concrete established. In the ground under the bedroom windowsill they discovered a footprint. Difficult to see, even with the two men shining their flashlights, only later, in daylight, would they gain any significant clues from it. Now, Oscar kneeling to inspect further, Cal held both flashlights tightly on the print, the only conclusive proof that someone had been lurking around the house earlier.

Next the amateur detectives moved to the living room window. First checking the ground for footprints, they found only Cal's from his earlier trip outside. If there had been prints, they had been erased by the big man's own feet. The marks on the bottom of the windowsill were still present, providing further evidence that someone had forced the window open, or at least had attempted to. The deputy wrote these two notes in his book and began to follow Cal back into his house.

Alice remained sitting with Nancy, who was feeling better, but still lying on the couch, trying to sip her tea. They saw the two men outside looking at the windowsill with their flashlights, wondering how someone could've been stealthy enough to open the window unnoticed. Nancy had been in the chair sitting less than three feet from the sill, and yet she heard nothing. It made her uneasy to consider that a stranger had been observing her for an undetermined length of time. What would make a person do such a thing, she wondered? Well, at least her daughter hadn't been affected by the poison gas.

Cal returned inside with Oscar, looking better than he had been before. His nerves were calmer, which helped the tension in the room decrease to an acceptable degree. Oscar instructed the Huffmans to go to bed and said he'd send Sheriff Mundy over in the morning to investigate further, although in truth, he felt there was very little to investigate. Perhaps a nighttime prowler had awakened the family's imagination, but nothing out of the ordinary beyond that. Biding them all a good night, he left the house and returned to his patrol car, turning the key twice before the engine turned over successfully. Oscar pulled out of the driveway, watching the house grow smaller and smaller in his rearview mirror, driving slowly until he saw the lights go out, then proceeding back to the sheriff station. His watch read 1:06.

All three members of the Huffman family settled down for an uneasy sleep. As Cal turned off the lights in the living room, he heard Nancy let out a shrill scream from the bedroom. Shocked, he turned back on the light and found his wife sitting on the bed in hysterics. The window was open and a breeze was cold blowing in, but he could not smell the gas that had stricken them earlier. Telling Nancy to calm down, holding her close to his chest with both hands, he kept asking her what happened. It was obvious the gasser had returned by the open window, but it didn't appear he had sprayed any gas this time.

Finally consoling Nancy, Cal closed the window and went into Alice's room to make sure she had gone back to bed all right. Opening the door to her room, he was almost knocked to the floor by the overpowering fumes that Alice's room was filled with. Leaving the lights off, for fear of igniting the gas,

Cal lifted his daughter and brought her safely from her bedroom to the living room. He set her down on the couch and tried to wake her up. Although it was only a matter of minutes between the deputy leaving and the family retiring to their beds, Cal found it impossible to wake her up.

He called for Nancy, and upon seeing her daughter lying unconscious on the couch, she relapsed into a fit of hysterics. Cal's head was swimming from having inhaled so much of the gas in Alice's room, but he managed to call the sheriff's office once again while Nancy tended to their daughter, who was still non-responsive.

There was no answer at the sheriff station; the deputy was still in his patrol car driving back. In fact, unbeknownst to Mr. Huffman, Oscar was still on Haymakertown Road driving towards Fincastle. The gasser had been watching, waiting for the deputy to leave before finishing the nefarious act.

After receiving no answer from the sheriff, Cal called his friend Kent Henderson who lived right down the road and asked him to come over right away, careful not to tell him the circumstances, but stressing that there was trouble at the house and they needed help. Once again, Cal was frantic, seeing his daughter in the state she was in tore him apart. It was even worse to not know whether or not she would recover from having breathed the noxious gas.

While waiting for Kent to make the short journey over, Cal phoned the family's doctor, Steven Driver. Not really accustomed to being awakened in the middle of the night, Dr. Driver was less than cordial on the phone. Mrs. Driver was even less so, after having received a stern lecture from the good doctor on how precious his sleep was and how he couldn't be running off into the night every time one of his patients had a minor cough. He assumed this from the fact that Cal was coughing from the effects of the gas. The doctor, not willing to be bothered with such a mundane problem, told Mr. Huffman to gargle a glass of salt water and call him in the morning.

Furious, Cal hung up the phone and returned to Alice's side. Nancy was coughing as she applied a warm compress to her daughter's forehead. This night had easily been the most bizarre in the family's immediate history, and none of them were taking it too well. Cal made another pot of tea, hoping that Kent would arrive sooner than later. He rang the sheriff's office while waiting for the water to boil, impatiently tapping his fingers on doorframe leading from the kitchen into the living room.

Finally, Oscar picked up on the other end. He understood Mr. Huffman's saying that a third gas attack happened right after the deputy's car was out of sight and the family members were tucked into their beds. Nothing Cal was saying really registered in Oscar's mind as important, or different from the story he reported earlier. When asked if everyone was all right, Cal told him Alice's condition, that she was totally unconscious, and that the doctor wouldn't come out because it was too late. The night's events fresh in his mind, the deputy agreed to make a return trip and to bring the doctor with him.

Calling Dr. Driver, Oscar insisted that he get out of bed and meet him at the Huffman residence. There was a young girl who had fallen seriously ill and needed medical attention. The deputy's story was ample cause to rise Driver from his slumber, and after changing into his clothes and grabbing his house-call medical bag, the doctor was out the door and driving towards his patient's home.

After finishing his conversation with Dr. Driver, Deputy Lemon jumped in his patrol car and, sirens blaring, took off towards Haymakertown Road. He was driving faster than usual, but he trusted that the siren and light would scare off any deer that happened to be wandering along the road in search of safe passage.

By the time Oscar arrived at the Huffman home, Kent was already there. As the patrol car pulled into the driveway, he and Cal came off the porch, both shouting and pointing east in the direction of the woods. They told him that shortly after Kent came, they heard a tapping sound coming from Alice's bedroom and when they entered to investigate, Cal thought he saw the figure of a man dressed in dark clothing running through the yard and away into the woods. Running out onto the porch, intending to give chase, the phantom prowler was nowhere to be seen. Cal wanted to set off in pursuit through the woods, but Kent wisely determined the idea to be too unsafe.

All three men went inside the house to wait for Dr. Driver. His house was in Troutville, and it was at least a twenty-minute drive after the doctor quit complaining to his wife about being awakened and managed to dress himself and get out the door.

Nancy was quietly tending to her daughter on the couch. Alice's legs were fully extended and her feet were propped up on the armrest opposite her head. The position of her body and the lack of panties under her slip afforded Kent a quick glance at her womanhood. It had been too many years since he had seen a naked woman, so he figured it wouldn't hurt to take a look while he had the opportunity. Lucky for him, the other people in the room were too absorbed with the problem at hand to notice his wandering eyes.

Cal and Oscar kept continual watch over the house, moving from window to window ensuring that all were securely fastened and squinting to see past the reflective pane into the darkness of the night. It was too dark outside to allow the men to see much farther than a few feet and as Cal moved closer to the windowpane, Oscar realized that the gasser could break the window and spray the poison right in their unsuspecting faces. The idea of gaping outside into the unknown night suddenly seemed very unappealing to the deputy and he joined the others in the living room.

Being in a ill-tempered mood, Dr. Driver opened the front door of the Huffman home on his own accord and entered without being asked to. Cal and the deputy both tried explaining the situation to Driver at the same time, then Nancy tried to add her part and finally Kent raised his voice to tell of the prowler Cal thought he saw. Unable to take the barrage of dialogue from the four, Dr. Driver told them all to be silent in a rather crude fashion and when they were quiet, he asked to see the girl.

Kneeling beside her on the floor, Driver took out his stethoscope and pressed it to her chest. After listening carefully for a few moments, he determined that her pulse was extremely weak and asked what had happened to her, allowing only her mother to answer the question. Nancy explained that Alice's room had been full of a strange gas and all of the family had breathed it, but Alice appeared to have inhaled the most.

Wasting no time, fearing for the girl's life, Dr. Driver immediately pulled the oxygen self-breather from his medical bag and placed the cup over the girl's mouth and nose. The doctor had only used this device twice before tonight and both had been drowning cases. The self-breather worked successfully in those cases, allowing oxygen to pump into the lungs, helping to kick-start the body into breathing independently again. Shortly after beginning the procedure, Alice was awake, although not entirely coherent. She tried to speak, but Dr. Driver told her to save her breath and just relax for a moment. Cal and Nancy hugged each other and breathed a sigh of relief that their daughter would be all right. Checking her pulse and heartbeat again, Driver found her to be coming out of her episode. As he placed his medical instruments back into his bag, the Huffmans fawned attention on their daughter.

Looking up from his bag, the doctor pulled Deputy Lemon into the kitchen and asked to know the details of the events leading up to the unconsciousness of the young girl. Oscar told him all that he knew, which wasn't very much. He was convinced that there had been a prowler of some kind lurking around the house that night, and that the assailant had sprayed gas into Huffman's house.

While the two professionals worked over the details of the case, Kent offered to spend the rest of the night at the house in case the attacker returned in the night. Rather suddenly, Alice lapsed into a fit of convulsions causing her to fall off the couch and into her mother's arms. Nancy called out for the doctor, and all four men in the house came to her aid. The doctor held Alice upright, trying to see if her airway was restricted or if there were an unseen problem causing the seizures.

A few moments later, the convulsions subsided, and Alice was normal again, although she complained of a sore throat and had some difficulty speaking. She did manage to drink the glass of water her father gave her and swallowed some pills Dr. Driver put into her shaking hand. Fearful of a relapse in her condition, Driver stayed at the house for another hour before leaving Alice in her bedroom asleep with Nancy sitting in a chair at her bedside watching over her.

Kent and Cal saw the doctor and deputy to their cars, all the while scanning the woods for any sign of the gasser. Oscar advised both men to stay in the house for the remainder of the evening, and to call the station if anything else happened, assuring them that Sheriff Mundy would be by in the morning. Doctor Driver handed Cal a bottle of pills for Alice and wished him luck, apologizing for not have come when first called.

The two men drove away one at a time and Cal and Kent returned to the house. They turned off all the lights, to aid their night vision and each took turns patrolling around the perimeter carrying Cal's rifle. If the gasser came back to attack again, there would be two armed men who were ready for anything.

Safe in her bedroom, resting comfortably in her slip beneath the covers, Alice drifted peacefully off to sleep with her mother watching over her, drinking a final cup of tea before going to sleep herself.

When morning came, the sun rose and pierced the darkness, vanquishing the terrors of the preceding night. Cal and Kent were both asleep in the living room, the husband on his couch and the friend in the chair by the window. Cal's rifle was lying on the floor beside him, his large hand resting on the butt. Everything was calm and serene.

A family of deer sprinted across the yard, their hooves making prints in the frosty ground. The sun shone brightly through the tops of the leafless trees, warming the isolated farmhouse and its inhabitants. Kent's car remained in the driveway parked next to Cal's. Both windshields were frosted over, and as the sun crept higher and higher, it began to melt the icy coating covering the glass.

Although usually early risers, everyone in the Huffman residence was still sleeping at seven o'clock when Sheriff Mundy's patrol car pulled into the driveway. Oscar Lemon stepped out of the passenger side while Dr. Driver and Dr. Breckinridge exited the car from the back seat doors. Deputy Lemon knocked on the door. Peering into the porch window, he could see two men asleep in the living room and tried to open the door, but found it locked.

Knocking again, harder this time, his gloved hand pounding on the heavy door, he was able to stir Cal Huffman, who answered with a groggy hello. The four men followed Cal into his living room and sat waiting while Kent, Cal and the two women got themselves ready for the morning company.

Doctor Samuel Driver had already recounted the medical aspects of the attack to his colleague Dr. William Beckenridge, the county medical examiner. Both doctors were eager to visit the house and check the progress of young Alice's condition. They were equally as eager to find the source of the mysterious gas that was reported in the house that evening.

A man both short and stout in comparison to Driver, William Breckinridge was hired as the county medical examiner seven years ago at the behest of the board of county supervisors after the man who previously held his position succumbed to the elements while hunting for elk in Colorado. The job wasn't very demanding, although the occasional murder did give him an opportunity to perform his duties. He still held a private practice and saw his patients on a schedule that suited him.

After all, with the extra income provided by the county job, William could afford to be selective about his clientele.

Breckinridge was a camp surgeon during the Great War, having been drafted, like many other doctors, for "a term of service not to extend past a cease-fire with the Germans." Like Kent, he only spent one year serving, but William never left the United States, instead serving with a medical platoon in Georgia tending to wounded soldiers coming in from the front. The money he saved allowed him to set up a small medical practice in his hometown of Fincastle after the war.

Now he listened to Alice's breathing with a stethoscope. The young girl was in her bedroom, where the two doctors were performing cursory medical examinations of the three Huffmans. While Alice was in her bedroom, Cal and Nancy were repeating their story to Sheriff Mundy. Kent gave his statement first and then went home to take care of some business, saying he would return later in the night to help watch over the house.

After her medical exam was done, Alice emerged from her bedroom and Dr. Driver called for Nancy to come in next. The sheriff asked Alice to sit on the couch next to her father. He proceeded to question her about the evening's events. Had she heard anything outside her window? Could she see anyone outside? When did she first smell the gas?

In truth, Alice had to admit that she was asleep or unconscious and only woke up when her father came rushing in to save her. She next remembered waking up in the living room with her parents and Dr. Driver standing over her. The gas made her throat tight and she felt dizzy and sick for several hours after being resuscitated. Her mouth still felt rather dry, and she continued to ask for glass after glass of water. Sometimes, it felt as though her tongue was swelling and if she didn't do something, it would fill her mouth completely, making it impossible to talk.

She could remember nothing of the attack, nor did she have any memory of the gas filling the room. As for the two attacks that occurred earlier that evening, her parents didn't wake her up until after Deputy Lemon was notified of the situation. All in all, her testimony proved rather useless to the investigation. While the medical examiner was slowly gaining a better understanding of the weapon, the lawmen were totally clueless as to the identity of the perpetrator.

Cal's statements proved much more useful. He told the sheriff about the chip marks on the windowsill, the footprint outside the house and the dark figure he thought he saw fleeing from his daughter's bedroom window. However, Cal neglected to mention anything of the stalker who had visited him three nights ago while walking home from Kent's house. Alice also didn't feel inclined to tell Sheriff Mundy about the strange woman she had seen watching her from the ridge beside the road several days ago. It just didn't seem relevant, as the two events seemed to have nothing to do with each other.

While being questioned, Alice was far from calm and collective. Her hands shook almost constantly, but the doctors attributed her current condition to shock and anxiety more than residual symptoms from the gas. Concluding their examination of Nancy, the doctors emerged from the bedroom and gave the family a clean bill of health. Whatever the gas was, its effects were apparently intense, but short term.

The sheriff and his deputy wanted to take a walk around the house and yard to see if they could uncover any clues besides those already found. Looking closely at the windowsill through which the gas was first sprayed, neither the sheriff nor the doctors could find any trace of residue. There were no markings on the inside from where the attacker lifted the window. The same went for the bedroom and Alice's room, no markings or residue on any of the windowsills.

Not content that a stove malfunction was the root of the problem, Mundy next went into the kitchen and instructed Deputy Lemon to pull the stove away from the wall to allow closer inspection. The pipes and fitting all appeared to be in good working order, no cracks or chips. Cal remarked that he had the pipes replaced after they smelled gas last summer, and they'd had no problems since then.

Moving the stove back into place, Cal continued to explain that he had smelled no gas when he entered the kitchen, while the gas was very pungent in the living room. Shaking his head unhappily, Sheriff Mundy paused, turning over the problem in his head. Rubbing the thinning brown hair gracing his crown, he glanced up at the other people in the room with him, taking in the looks on their faces.

Cal and Nancy were convinced that they had been gassed. His deputy also appeared to be convinced that some kind of attack had taken place during the night. The doctors were both noncommittal, judging by the expressions of amazement while comparing notes. Nothing like this had ever happened before in Botetourt County, or in any county for that matter. The only thing Sheriff Mundy knew about gas attacks were stories he heard from veterans returning from the Great War, and those took place a continent away.

The sheriff and his entourage walked out to the porch, Cal leading the way around the side of the house to the living room window from where the gas seemed to emanate. It was a cold morning, but the fresh sunlight pouring over the hills heated their exposed faces and made the trip outside tolerable, if not a little pleasant. Moving through the yard, they saw the prints left by the deer at sunup.

Country air is different than air anywhere else, and nothing else can compare to it. It's always fresh and it fills the lungs with scents of flowers, wheat, bark and soil. Clean air, good air. In the mornings, this unique smell is intensified because the lungs are accustomed to breathing the stale scent of the indoors. Dew and frost coat the ground, giving the entire picture a pristine radiance, glistening in the morning sun.

Looking closely at the damage on the windowsill, Sheriff Mundy asked Cal when he last painted the house. Thinking back, he realized it had been two springs ago. The temperature was unusually high that year in March, so he took

154

the opportunity to paint the entire house over the course of a week. The scrape marks could have been made between then and now, so Mundy wasted no more time inspecting them.

Deputy Lemon was standing over the footprint by the bedroom window. The doctors, Cal and Mundy all kneeled down on the frozen grass, taking care not to disturb the delicate print. Whereas darkness obscured the print's dimensions, by the light of day, much could be divined from the depth and shape. It appeared to be the imprint of a woman's shoe, the high-heeled kind that neither Nancy nor Alice owned. Cal assured the sheriff that no other female caller had been at the Huffman home in the last week or so. Doctor Breckinridge made a sketch and recorded the dimensions of the print for future use with the sheriff's office.

As strange as the print was, it lent no conclusive proof to anything. The idea that a lone woman was stalking through the woods, spraying toxic gas in the homes of country residents while wearing high heels was simply absurd. To Sheriff Mundy, the very idea of a gas attack was beyond absurd, and he felt the whole business should be wrapped up as quickly as possible. While he could produce no viable explanation for the family's earlier condition, they appeared to be fine now.

Mundy was prepared to write the whole incident off as a non-event, preparing the statement in his mind before he formally declared it to his companions. Whatever had happened last night was indeed bizarre, but couldn't be confirmed as a case of assault. Walking back to the front of the house, the group saw Nancy standing beside the porch, bent over looking at something.

Mrs. Huffman's gaze was fixed upon the high-heel print beside the front porch. Bending down to investigate further, the tracks led under the porch and stopped in the center. How odd, she thought, that someone would want to crawl under there wearing their best shoes, shoes that were too nice for her to own, let alone go trouncing around the dirt in. After considering all the possibilities for the appearance of the tracks and arriving at no reasonable explanation, Nancy began to wave at the men approaching her, beckoning them to move quicker.

While she was hunkered down, the men came up beside Nancy and began an inquiry into her discovery. There were four sets of footprints in the loose dirt under the porch. It seemed that whoever had made them was squatting down, shuffling to get further and further out of sight. It was fairly obvious to the men that whoever had been standing at the window was the same person that made the tracks leading under the porch, and furthermore, in all likelihood, that person had been hiding there for some presumably nefarious reason.

Back in the house, Cal and Nancy said nothing to their daughter about the discoveries outside. A young girl who had been recently traumatized — there was no reason to trouble her mind with such things. Alice remained in her bed for the rest of the morning and most of the afternoon, taking tea when her mother brought it and eating biscuits for lunch.

Doctor Driver wanted the Huffmans to stop by his office in a few days for a checkup, just to make sure that there were no persistent symptoms, and to ensure that Alice's condition didn't worsen. Both doctors bid their farewells and headed for the patrol car. Sheriff Mundy sent Oscar to go warm up the engine and wait with the doctors while he discussed things with Cal.

Standing in the doorway, Mundy's face was somewhere between friendliness and contempt. When Cal asked what his family should do next, the sheriff leaned in and told him not to worry, it was probably an isolated incident, just a freak thing that happens now and again. Most likely some kids messing around. Cal shrugged his shoulders and accepted what he had been told. Sheriff Mundy tipped his hat and headed towards his patrol car as Cal closed the door.

The four men drove back to Fincastle in relative silence. The doctors were looking over their notes and Deputy Lemon stared vacantly out the window, daydreaming about hunting trips and fishing in the roadside brook. He was feeling more than a little tired, his shift had officially ended at six that

156

morning, but he'd agreed to accompany the sheriff to assist with the investigation at the Huffman's. Oscar dozed off and on throughout the ride.

Without comparing their notes, the doctors already knew they had no difference of opinion concerning the direct facts of the case. Their patients were very obviously the victims of a traumatic event, and Alice's earlier symptoms as recorded by Dr. Driver mirrored those of gas inhalation victims Dr. Breckinridge had treated during the war.

Sheriff Mundy was convinced there was a logical explanation to the whole matter. It seemed easy to attribute the whole incident to local kids, but the presence of the woman's high-heel shoe print was just too strange. It didn't fit with the rest of the puzzle. The entire thing just seemed bizarre, out of place for a small rural area, certainly not the kind of activity one would expect to occur with any frequency in the woods of Western Virginia.

Because he was a reasonable, practical man, when he came up against something he couldn't understand, Mundy used his practical line of thinking to solve the problem. In the eight years since he had been elected to the office of sheriff, there remained no unsolved cases in Botetourt County. Not that there was usually much detective work required for the cases that he investigated, but nevertheless, his record had to count for something.

Lawrence Mundy was born and raised in Botetourt County, his family owned several businesses in Fincastle and it was through his father's connections that he was able to win the election for sheriff. Overall, Mundy was considered an honest and approachable man. He wasn't adverse to being awakened in the middle of the night to settle a dispute between two neighbors feuding over a trifle. While his practical thinking forced skepticism to seep into the cracks of his mind on this case, he still considered himself more than competent to handle the investigation.

Pulling in at the sheriff's office, the four men exited the vehicle and stood in the parking lot to the rear of the building talking about the next course of action, which as everyone seemed to agree, was to hope that this was a one time event. And barring the continuation of further attacks, nothing would be said to the press. In the meantime, the doctors could attempt to determine the nature of the gas used while Sheriff Mundy would set about questioning the parents of known troublemakers to see where their children had been during the time of the attacks. On a Friday night, it was more than likely most people would be unable to account for their children's actual whereabouts.

Doctor Breckinridge entered the sheriff's office first, heading straight to the typewriter to begin his report. Doctor Driver headed to his car and went home prepared to make up the sleep that he lost during the night, compounded further by Mundy waking him at six in the morning to accompany the investigation team. The sheriff told his deputy to leave his notebook with Dr. Breckinridge and go home, further explaining that he could come in two hours late to make up for the overtime he put in this morning. Lemon thanked him and proceeded down the street towards his house.

Sitting in the room usually occupied by the sheriff's secretary, Breckinridge was diligently typing his report. Both his and Driver's notebooks were laid open on the desk beside him, in silent competition for terrible penmanship. As he recounted the events described by the victims, he began to feel great empathy towards them. A toxic gas had been sprayed by an unknown assailant on an unsuspecting family. Hands banging the keys, he tried to imagine how he and his own family might react under the same circumstances.

Picturing his wife in Nancy's place, and his son Lomax in Alice's, the doctor realized that if the attacks were carried out by more than mischievous adolescents, every family in Botetourt County might be in danger. There would be no telling where the gasser might strike next; everyone would be vulnerable to attack. It wasn't like being at war, where gas masks and decontamination kits are issued to soldiers who are expecting to be attacked with chemical munitions. This enemy was using guerrilla tactics, targeting civilians, and it would be extremely difficult to find the perpetrator, especially if he and Dr. Driver were unable to determine the composition of the gas.

To deduce the type of gas, Breckinridge first had to rule out what it was not. The gas was unlikely to be of military grade, it was more likely something that could be easily purchased or obtained without much trouble. Chloroform was his first consideration, but Cal Huffman would've been knocked unconscious when he raced into Alice's bedroom to rescue his daughter. Also, it was unlikely that Nancy would've reported the gas in the living room as smelling "like gas," since chloroform has a unique odor that is difficult to confuse with anything else.

Deputy Lemon had raised the possibility of ether, but this also has a distinctive smell that the victims would've reported. Additionally, their symptoms didn't match those of patients that Breckinridge had treated for overexposure to the solvent. In almost all of his ether exposure cases, the most common problem was prolonged lack of breath and sometimes dizziness. Even in the worst cases, symptoms rarely went beyond blurred vision, but were never as extreme as total loss of consciousness.

It was Alice's unconsciousness that caused him to rule out Mundy's suggestion of tear gas. While training for the medical corps during his time in the military, Breckinridge had observed a group of soldiers during their last stages of basic training. On one occasion, they were undergoing instruction on how to behave in a chemical environment. In the doctor's understanding, this was one of the most unpleasant phases of their basic training, but a necessary one now that the Germans were using chemical weapons on the open battle field.

A group of one hundred and fifty recruits stood in formation in a large airtight room lined with glass windows to accommodate outside observation. Doctor Breckinridge stood there with his colleagues as row after row of would-be soldiers assembled in formation, holding their gas masks in their hands. The facilitator instructed them to don their masks and wait for further instructions. While they were doing this, he told them that they must learn to trust that their gas masks would protect them in a chemical environment, and that they were going to be exposed to CS gas, a harassing agent which is basically military-grade tear gas.

When all the recruits were wearing their gas masks, the facilitator put his on and produced what appeared to be a large pill. He placed the pill on a hotplate, and the recruit's eyes widened as white gas poured slowly from the burning pill. The facilitator took a small electric fan and began to blow the gas throughout the room, flooding it completely. He then instructed the first row of recruits to take one step forward and remove their gas masks.

Immediately after exposing themselves, the recruits were all choking madly, their eyes watering and their noses running uncontrollably. Giving them a few minutes to soak up the gas, the facilitator opened the side door leading outside and ordered them to leave. Each one following the other, all trying desperately to see and fighting to breathe, they worked their way out of the room. Staring in disbelief, watching the unfortunate first rank exit, the other recruits were suddenly not prepared to remove their gas masks. Their fear was intensified when the facilitator closed the door and dropped another gas pill on the hotplate.

It was obvious to Dr. Breckinridge that tear gas was not the agent used by whomever had gassed the Huffmans. Tear gas causes a burning sensation on every portion of the body it comes into contact with. Skin, eyes, nose and throat all become like searing coals, and Alice would've been awakened after taking one breath of the vile stuff. It's also unlikely that her parents would've been able to remain in the house after three separate attacks. The training room Breckinridge visited still reeked of gas twenty minutes after the last recruit had fled.

There were several other options for him to discount, but most of them seemed highly unreasonable to suggest. Numerous types of military-grade gas could cause the symptoms experienced by the Huffman family. The most notable would be chlorine or maybe phosgene gas. Both are choking agents and their corrosive effect on the respiratory system usually results in pulmonary edema, filling the lungs with fluid and ultimately choking the victim to death. Of course, phosgene is more effective than chlorine because it is slowly hydrolyzed by the water in the lining of the lungs, forming hydrochloric acid, rapidly destroying the tissue.

The symptoms exhibited by the Huffmans closely matched those of mild exposure to a military-grade choking agent. Coughing, nausea, headache, fatigue, but once again, Alice wouldn't have been knocked unconscious by the attack, she would've been awakened and forced from the room by a desire to breathe. Although, if enough of the gas had been sprayed into her room in a short period of time, she may have passed out due to a simple lack of oxygen. On the other hand, Cal's reaction was rather mild, if the room had been full of a choking agent, he would've had lasting damage to his nose and throat, as would young Alice.

Other military-grade chemical weapons simply didn't fit the bill. While popular during the war, mustard gas not only has a distinct smell, but even in non-lethal doses it leaves small blisters where it contacts with skin. There were no such blisters discovered on any of the victims. Besides, mustard gas is a persistent agent, and the investigators would've found traces of it in the room or at least on the window through which it was sprayed. Considering his options, Dr. Breckinridge continued to turn the gas question over in his head while moving on to the medical notes.

Reviewing his and Dr. Driver's notes, he carefully typed the victim's symptoms into the official report: *The victims*

*experienced nausea accompanied by a headache. In addition,
the mother and daughter had difficulty speaking because their
mouth and throat muscles were constricted. While this could
have been caused by a lack of oxygen, it is more likely to be an
effect of the gas used in the attack. One victim suffered
convulsions after being resuscitated by Dr. Driver. The doctor
could not determine the cause of the seizures beyond
overexposure to the gas. Her parents did not experience
convulsions, nor a loss of consciousness, however, they did not
breathe as much of the gas as their daughter. It is unlikely that
Alice Huffman's extreme condition was caused by anxiety,
although she was very obviously in a state of near-shock when
examined after the attack. I conclude that her initial
unconsciousness and later convulsions were a direct result of
her exposure to the gas.*

Now that he had boiled down the attack to a series of
raw facts and their logical conclusions, it was time to attempt
piecing together the details, a job for the sheriff and his
investigators. The doctor's job as a medical examiner was all
but complete. He removed the report from the typewriter and
signed the bottom with an ink pen, writing the date along the
left edge of the paper to aid the secretary in her cross-reference
filing system. Placing the report into a manila folder,
Breckinridge took his jacket off the hanger in the closet and
proceeded down the hall to Mundy's office.

The sheriff was in the middle of a phone conversation
when Dr. Breckinridge entered without knocking. He sat
quietly in a chair in front of Mundy's desk until the phone call
was over. Sheriff Mundy was talking to his wife about their
plans for dinner that evening, and more specifically, what their
dinner would consist of. While Mundy was insisting that they
eat steaks or liver, his wife seemed to be demanding chicken.
As the argument intensified, their speech getting sterner but not
louder, Dr. Breckinridge was suddenly compelled to leave the
room, dropping his jacket as he did so.

Back in the secretary's office, he removed his report on the attack from the manila folder and slid it back into the typewriter. Typing furiously now, as though driven on by some unseen conductor, Breckinridge completed a few short lines and paused, almost exhausted by the effort. He looked up at his words, and was amazed by their content, as though a writer of great clout had swept into the room and picked up where he left off. It was now very clear to him what the gas might be, and he spoke the theory aloud to himself as he returned to Sheriff Mundy's office.

When the doctor entered again, once again without knocking, he took the phone from Mundy's hand and said thank you to his wife before hanging it up. Chagrined, the sheriff sat speechless, waiting for what he hoped was a good explanation for the doctor's actions.

Barely able to control his excitement, Breckinridge began recounting a story about two men who had entered his office one night as he was getting ready to close. The older man was supporting the younger as he limped through the door and sat down in the waiting area. Surprised by the late-night patients, the doctor explained that he was closed, and would see them in the morning unless it was an emergency.

The older man stepped forward and confessed that he and his friend had been out stealing chickens when the tin can they were using to hold the chicken gas broke and suffocated the younger man. Doctor Breckinridge stood staring at the two men, not knowing what to think. After looking the man over, listening to his breathing, he started to ask questions about the business of chicken theft.

Seeing that his friend would be safe in the doctor's hands, the older man began to explain his profession in a matter-of-fact fashion. Chicken thieving, as he called it, was conducted at night, and the quickest and easiest way to abduct the chickens without arousing the owner was to pour a little "chicken gas" into their coop, and then abduct the unconscious foul. When asked about the composition of this gas, the man was unwilling to lend any details, only insisting on learning whether or not his friend would recover.

Doctor Breckinridge assured him that his friend would be just fine, and allowed the men to leave. A shady legal matter, perhaps, but the doctor had a great deal of sympathy for the poor of the area who were forced to scrape together a living during the great depression. The symptoms the young man exhibited matched those of the Huffman family, although not exactly. Breckinridge had no opportunity to question the man in detail about his medical condition, but the two cases appeared to be similar.

The sheriff was more than familiar with chicken gas. In fact, the two men Breckinridge had described were sitting in the jail next door and would remain there for another five days. He could buy the theory of the gas, but not the motive. While the Huffmans owned a good deal of chickens, none of them had been stolen, eliminating burglary. Perhaps it was time to consider revenge, the doctor thought. Mundy was still confident that the whole thing was nothing more than teenage pranksters. Sure, they may have used chicken gas, but that didn't make them violent offenders. By his estimation, the whole thing would become a non-event and be forgotten in a matter of days. It was December 23rd, and Christmas was just around the corner.

Unfortunately for the residents of Botetourt County, so was another gas attack.

EPILOGUE

Staring Into the Abyss

"Man looks into the abyss. There's nothing looking back at him. That's when man finds his character, and that's what keeps him from falling into the abyss."
-Wall Street

Most paranormal investigators who are active in the field attempt at some time or another to write a book about their experiences and theories. Those who do not fall into one of two categories: either they are not inclined to write, or they keep saying "I'll write a book when reports stop coming in and my investigations calm down." However, paranormal events are always happening, and thus most investigators are simply too busy to dedicate the time required to writing a decent book.

Quite literally, in the days following the final edit of *Into the Abyss* by a freelance editor, I was back on the trail in pursuit of the unknown. Hence, this volume is already in need of updating and I will attempt a brief addendum here.

Several of Dr. Santee's close colleagues have since contacted me and offered new information, mostly backing up what I have already uncovered about the good doctor. Although one former friend stated that Santee's first wife was not schizophrenic, but that Frederick used to say "everyone is schizophrenic."

I have discovered that there was actually a gas attack that predated the 1933 Botetourt attacks. In Columbus, Georgia in 1926, there were a series of three gas attacks in three weeks. The local paper stated that robbery was the motive. Perhaps the gasser was truly mad and moved from state to state over the course of nearly twenty years. So far as I know, I am the first researcher to bring these old/new attacks to light, and more research must be done on those cases.

A two-night excursion into Rickett's Glen State Park in early September 2006 proved very, very successful. My team actually had two encounters with what we believe was a Bigfoot. I came closer than ever to seeing one of the magnificent creatures, although it was obscured by heavy forest cover. I can now say from personal experience that they do smell quite horrible.

It has recently been suggested to me that the three-toed track given to Eric Altman was possibly faked, although there is no conclusive evidence to support this. Besides, the fact that it is nearly identical to the track found in Ohio makes me think that they're from the same creature.

★   ★   ★

In closing, it should be noted that the pursuit of the paranormal can be an obsessive, frustrating, and even dangerous endeavor. The weak in spirit will not last long when confronted by forces they cannot hope to understand, and quickly give up; while the noble-minded will try to persevere against conventional science and shrug off derision from their family, friends, and colleagues.

The truly dedicated paranormal investigator will keep staring at something they can't see until it consumes them against their very will, and at that moment, they shall find what they seek.

Appendix A
U.S. Bigfoot Sightings by State

Alabama	32
Alaska	18
Arizona	23
Arkansas	58
California	324
Colorado	77
Connecticut	3
Delaware	2
Florida	76
Georgia	25
Hawaii	0
Idaho	39
Illinois	49
Indiana	43
Iowa	35
Kansas	26
Kentucky	45
Louisiana	32
Maine	13
Maryland	25
Massachusetts	9
Michigan	62
Minnesota	25
Mississippi	12
Missouri	52
Montana	23
Nebraska	5
Nevada	6
New Hampshire	9
New Jersey	20
New Mexico	27
New York	73
North Carolina	34
North Dakota	5
Ohio	187
Oklahoma	59

Oregon	187
Pennsylvania	87
Rhode Island	2
South Carolina	24
South Dakota	11
Tennessee	47
Texas	152
Utah	31
Vermont	4
Virginia	23
Washington	378
West Virginia	26
Wisconsin	31
Wyoming	22

Appendix B
Project Blue Book Unknowns

Total UFO Sightings, 1947 - 1969

YEAR	TOTAL SIGHTINGS	UNIDENTIFIED
1947	122	12
1948	156	7
1949	186	22
1950	210	27
1951	169	22
1952	1,501	303
1953	509	42
1954	487	46
1955	545	24
1956	670	14
1957	1,006	14
1958	627	10
1959	390	12
1960	557	14
1961	591	13
1962	474	15
1963	399	14
1964	562	19
1965	887	16
1966	1,112	32
1967	937	19
1968	375	3
1969	146	1
TOTAL	12,618	701

Appendix C
Inventory of the Rhodes Excavation

A Site
A1: Sokwik dish detergent, rusted
A2: Small jar, glass, no lid
A3: Large glass Clorox container, brown
A4: Tobacco tin, very rusted
A5: Small bottle with lid on, rusted
A6: "Mecreca Liquid" can, very rusted
A7: Flask, glass with plastic lid

B Site
B1: Glass bottle found wedged between a rock and a tree

C Site
C1: Bottle of floor wax
C2: Bottle of floor wax
C3: Rusted tin can
C4: Rusted tin can

D Site
D1: Broken glass container with leaf design
D2: Areo Way containers (2), rusted
D3: Listerine bottle, glass
D4: Perfume bottle, glass
D5: Small jar, glass
D6: Sokwik container
D7: Velvet tobacco boxes (2), rusted
D8: Boraxo tin, rusted
D9: Tin container with lid, rusted
D10: Small square tin, rusted
D11: Vitalis bottle, glass
D12: Cylinder bottle with lid, glass, something white inside of it
D13-D14b: 3 tin cans, one inside the other with a perfectly preserved broken egg inside the smallest one, all rusted
D15: Blue bottle, glass, broken
D16: Pink glass vase, broken into 7 pieces
D17: Light transistor, broken

Appendix D
Botetourt County 1930 Census Data

Name	Residence	Birth Date	Rel to Head
Claude Huffman	Fincastle	abt 1896	Head
Nancy Huffman	Fincastle	abt 1902	Wife
Laurence H. Huffman	Fincastle	abt 1920	Son
Nellie Huffman	Fincastle	abt 1922	Daughter
Kenneth Huffman	Fincastle	abt 1925	Son
Alferd Huffman	Fincastle	abt 1927	Son
Luther M. Huffman	Fincastle	abt 1929	Son
Kent W. Henderson	Amsterdam	abt 1878	Head
Eva R. Henderson	Amsterdam	abt 1879	Wife
Katie E. Henderson	Amsterdam	abt 1901	Daughter
Ashby H. Henderson	Amsterdam	abt 1909	Son
Helen P. Henderson	Amsterdam	abt 1911	Daughter
Grover G. Henderson	Amsterdam	abt 1913	Son
Alice R. Cronise	Amsterdam	abt 1915	Niece
William J. Guy	Amsterdam	abt 1862	Head
Nancy C. Guy	Amsterdam	abt 1872	Wife
Ada K. Guy	Amsterdam	abt 1910	Daughter
Tiny B. Guy	Amsterdam	abt 1914	Daughter
Clinton T. Guy	Amsterdam	abt 1921	Grandson
Clarence Hall	Amsterdam	abt 1902	Son-in-law
Lucy Hall	Amsterdam	abt 1903	Daughter
Daniel Hall	Amsterdam	abt 1925	Grandson
Hattie Hall	Amsterdam	abt 1927	Gnddaughter
Daniel Hylton	Amsterdam	abt 187	Head
Martha A. Hylton	Amsterdam	abt 1875	Wife
Pauline D. Hylton	Amsterdam	abt 1918	Daughter
Emmit C. Lee	Amsterdam	abt 1885	Head
Lura G. Lee	Amsterdam	abt 1895	Wife
Bernice E. Lee	Amsterdam	abt 1919	Daughter
Vergie M. Lee	Amsterdam	abt 1921	Daughter
Thelma C. Lee	Amsterdam	abt 1923	Daughter

Norma L. Lee	Amsterdam	abt 1924	Daughter
Garland L. Lee	Amsterdam	abt 1926	Son
Emmit C. Lee	Amsterdam	abt 1927	Son
Andry L. Lee	Amsterdam	abt 1929	Daughter
William P. Moore	Salem	abt 1880	Head
Lucy Moore	Salem	abt 1905	Wife

SELECTED BIBLIOGRAPHY

Gorillas in Our Midst

Coleman, Loren. *Bigfoot! The True Story of Apes in America.*

Coleman, Loren. *Cryptozoology A to Z.*

Crabtree, Smokey. *Smokey and the Fouke Monster.*

Dahinden, Rene and Hunter, Don. *Sasquatch Bigfoot.*

Green, John. *On the Track of Sasquatch.*

Green, John. *Encounters With Bigfoot.*

Jurmain. *Essentials of Physical Anthropology.*

Krantz, Grover. *Bigfoot Sasquatch Evidence.*

Morgan, Robert W. *Bigfoot: the Ultimate Adventure.*

Morgan, Robert W. *The Bigfoot Pocket Field Guide.*

Rife, Philip J. *Bigfoot Across America.*

UFOs and Aliens

Berlitz, Charles. *The Roswell Incident.*

Dickinson, Terence. *The Zeta Reticuli Incident.*

Friedman, Stanton T. *A Review of Case MJ-12.*

Hawking, Stephen. *The Nature of Space and Time.*

Huyghe, Patrick. *The Field Guide to Extraterrestrials.*

Randle, Kevin D. *Case MJ-12.*

Randles, Jenny. *The Truth Behind the Men in Black.*

Things That Go Bump in the Night

Huyghe, Patrick. *The Field Guide to Ghosts and Other Apparitions.*

The Witch Doctor of Wapwallopen

Allen, George. History of William H. Allen, Bookseller, 1918-1997.

Bradsby, H.C. History of Luzerne County, Pa. N.p. 1893.

"Dr. Charles Santee, 88, Dies At His Home in Wapwallopen." Hazleton Standard-Speaker 17 Apr. 963.

"Frederick L. Santee." Chronicle Telegram 19 Jul. 1924.

"Genius Friend of Pastor." Gettysburg Star and Sentinel 02 Oct. 1920.

Gowan, John. Operations of Increasing Order. Northridge, CA: John C. Gowan, 1980.

"Is Boy Wonder." Gettysburg Star and Sentinel 28 Jul. 1923.

Hoke, G. Doctor Frederick LaMotte Santee. Harrisburg, PA: Zaxon, 1990.

"Local Scholar Dies in Wapwallopen." Bloom Times 12 Apr. 1980.

"Mrs. Betty Santee, 57 Writer and Poet, Dies." Bloom Times 23 Apr. 1962.

"Pennsylvania Boy of 13 is Admitted to Harvard." Scranton Times 11 Sep. 1920.

Rosenbaum, Ron. Explaining Hitler. NY: HarperPerennial, 1999.

Santee, Ephraim A. Ledgers, 1870-1905, 1870-1911. N.p. 1911.

Santee, Frederick L. The Devil's Wager. Hicksville, NY: Exposition Press, 1979.

The Mad Gasser of Botetourt County and The Gasser's First Victims

Clark, Jerome. *Strange and Unexplained Phenomena.*

Clark, Jerome. *Unexplained!*.

Johnson, D.M. *The "Phantom Anesthetist" of Mattoon: A field study of mass hysteria*. Journal of Abnormal and Social Psychology, 1945.

Maruna, Scott. *The Mad Gasser of Mattoon*.

ABOUT THE AUTHOR

A preeminent expert in all things paranormal, Travis McHenry was a dual major in theater and anthropology at Bloomsburg University (Pennsylvania) before leaving college early to work for the U.S. Navy as an intelligence analyst from 2001-2008.

He has lectured widely on the subject of Bigfoot evolution and migration, appeared on the television show *Creepy Canada*, and has been featured in such publications as *The Washington Post*, *The Norfolk Compass*, and *Chronogram* magazine.

For ten years, starting in 1997, Travis worked with a small team of field experts under the banner of the Paranormal Research-Response Team investigating mysteries in Pennsylvania and Virginia.

He announced his formal retirement from the field of paranormal investigation in 2007 to focus on his acting career, and can now be frequently found on stages in Los Angeles and Orange County.

Travis is the author of several books and plays, including *Tales of Terror*, *Delusions of Grandeur*, and the epic poem *In the Aftermath*.

You can contact Travis or learn more about him at www.travismchenry.com

Made in the USA
Lexington, KY
04 August 2014